Diversity and cohesion

**new challenges for
the integration of immigrants and minorities**

prepared for the Council of Europe
by Jan Niessen
Director of the Migration Policy Group
in co-operation with
the European Cultural Foundation

Directorate General III – Social Cohesion
Directorate of Social Affairs and Health

Council of Europe Publishing

French edition:

Diversité et cohésion: de nouveaux défis pour l'intégration des immigrés et des minorités

ISBN 92-871-4344-7

Cover design: Graphic Design Workshop of the Council of Europe

Council of Europe Publishing
F-67075 Strasbourg Cedex

ISBN 92-871-4345-5
© Council of Europe, July 2000
Printed in Germany

Table of contents

Preface by Václav Havel, President of the Czech Republic

Předmluva prezidenta České republiky Václava Havla
ke zprávě Rady Evropy

The Report on Diversity and Cohesion

Vážení Evropané,

byla-li kdy Evropa jednotná a nejednotná v jeden okamžik, pak je to právě nyní. Evropa je totiž kontinentem plným vyzrálých i zrajících národů a států, a také kontinentem, otevřený k přijetí všech, kteří si hledají nová místa k životu.

Evropa uměla a umí se otvírat nově přicházejícím. Bylo jejím darem i údělem v minulosti, že v sobě nesla mnohé z toho, po čem ti ostatní toužili nebo co hledali. Evropa přijímala mnoho z těch, kteří se k ní obraceli s nadějí z hlubin blízkých i vzdálených kontinentů a vždy hledala a hledá jejich místo mezi těmi, které sama zrodila. V uplynulém půlstoletí alespoň v jedné ze svých částí nacházela cestu k těm, kteří se liší proto, že jejich domovinou byl jiný světadíl. Evropa byla a měla by zůstat otevřeným kontinentem.

Druhá i třetí generace těch, kteří nalezli sílu či odpovědnost odpoutat se od svého vlastního domova či těch, kteří útěkem zachránili alespoň zbytek důstojnosti či vlastní život, nyní žije, doplňujíce ty domácí, v mnoha evropských zemích. Poselství jiných světů zakotvené v odlišnosti těchto kultur i jejich hodnotách nyní obohacuje mnohá evropská města i místa.

Současné a hluboce zakořeněné tradice Evropy jsou však opět na různých místech s dávkou nacionální arogance pošlapávány. Opřeni o ještě doutnající plynové komory snaží se někteří vrátit zpět to, po čem je nemožné truchlit. Krvavý souboj principů zřetelný v těch evropských částech, kde démoni minula nepoučeni rozhrabávají rozvaliny nacionalismu probíhá všude tam, kde jde o nové uspořádání věcí.

Konfrontace rovnosti a svobody, vysoké ceny každé lidské individuality s krvavou touhou po moci, nadřazenosti a elitářství však musí dát jasnou odpověď, co je to budoucnost a jaký je morální rozměr budoucnosti tohoto kontinentu.

Tato konfrontace probíhá v každém z nás v míře vlastní rezignace na temné minulosti a v aktivním odporu nerovnosti lidí. Dluhy z minulého či nedostatky odpovědnosti a velkorysosti k současnému plodí neduhy rasismu a xenofobie.

Tento osobní boj nesmí nikdo z nás prohrát nebo promarnit. Jen tak lze dát šanci vzájemnému vztahu člověka a člověka, porozumění, pochopení, toleranci a pokoře.

Václav Havel

Preface

Dear Europeans,

If ever Europe had been united and divided at the same time, it is precisely now. Because Europe is a Continent full of mature and maturing Nations and States, it is also a Continent open to welcome all people seeking a new place to live.

Europe knows, and has always known, how to open herself to newcomers. In the past, it was her gift, as well as her destiny that she carried within herself much of what others desired or searched for. Europe was receptive to many who turned towards her with hope, from the depths of the near or distant Continents of the world, and she found, and continues to find, a place for them to live amongst those she bore herself. During the last half century, Europe, at least in one of its corners, has been able to accommodate those who differed because their homeland was of another Continent. Europe was and should always remain an open Continent.

The second and the third generation – of those who found the strength or the responsibility to separate themselves from their own homes or those who escaped, and saved at least a residue of dignity or their own lives, – dwell here now – a complement to the original inhabitants of many European countries. The legacy from other parts of the world, anchored in the differences of cultures and their values, now enrich many European towns and environments.

Contemporary as well as deeply rooted European traditions are yet again, in different places, being trampled upon with a great deal of nationalistic arrogance. Some people try to return to that which is impossible to mourn for in leaning back on the still smoking gas chambers. A ferocious fight of principles – evident in those parts of Europe where the demons of the past, not having learned anything, still claw in the ruins of nationalism – is in progress in all those places where a new order has begun.

The confrontation between equality, freedom and the high cost of human individuality against a bloody thirst for power, superiority and elitism, however, must give us a clear answer about the meaning of the future, and what the moral dimension of what this Continent's future will be.

This confrontation takes place in each of us, to the extent of our own resignation of the dark past, and in the active resistance to the inequality of people. Past debts, or the lack of responsibility and generosity to the present, stir up the maladies of racism and xenophobia to the fore.

None of us must lose or forfeit this personal fight. In this way only, we can give a chance to a man to man reciprocal relationship, perception, under-standing, tolerance and humility.

Václav Havel
President of the Czech Republic

Introduction

Since its inception, 50 years ago, the Council of Europe has made democracy, human rights and the rule of law permanent priorities for Europe and has been committed to the defence of human dignity and the development of social progress.

The Heads of State and Government of the member States of the Council of Europe, meeting in Strasbourg for their second Summit in 1997, affirmed in their Final Declaration that social cohesion is one of the foremost needs of the wider Europe and should be pursued as an essential complement to the promotion of human rights and dignity. In this perspective, they also affirmed their determination to protect the rights of lawfully residing migrant workers[1] and to facilitate their integration in the societies in which they live. In the Plan of Action adopted by the Heads of State and Government, the Committee of Ministers was instructed i. a. to define a social cohesion strategy to respond to the challenges in society.

The European Ministers responsible for migration affairs, at their Sixth Conference in 1996, identified the integration of immigrants and minorities as one of the most important goal of public policy in all States with large, legally settled populations of foreign origin.

Recognising the importance of the contribution made by the Council of Europe to reflection and practice in the field of integration and community relations, the Ministers requested the European Committee on Migration (CDMG) to prepare a major report drawing on the report on Community and ethnic relations in Europe from 1991, but reflecting more recent developments and the widening membership of the Council of Europe.

The newer member States of the Council of Europe in many cases comprise large "national minorities". Strengthening the protection of national minorities is an activity directly stemming from the Vienna Summit in 1993, which was subsequently reaffirmed at the Strasbourg Summit in 1997. There has been a gradual development of programmes to help the various national communities establish relationships based on mutual trust. It is self-evident that the principles of community relations are of considerable relevance in this context too.

On the occasion of the recent 50th anniversary of the Council of Europe, the Committee of Ministers committed the organisation to continue combating

---

1. There was a consensus among CDMG members not to tackle the issue of irregular migration

the divisive factors constituted by racism, xenophobia, political, cultural or religious intolerance and discrimination against minorities. They also expressed their will to build on the community of culture formed by a Europe enriched by its diversity, confident in its identity and open to the world.

The present report on "Diversity and cohesion in a changing Europe" sets as a basic principle that integration of immigrants and national minorities is one of the pillars of social cohesion. The report is based on a thorough review of community relations policies carried out on behalf of the European Committee on Migration in the majority of the Council of Europe member States. The forward-looking responses to these findings, as sketched out in the report, fit perfectly in the new overall priorities defined for the organisation as such:

- The importance of a continued action on a national level through co-operation, technical assistance and legal expertise in a comparative approach.
- The identification of NGOs and local partners in the implementation of the intergovernmental programme of activities.
- The provision of effective and adapted assistance to face challenges to social cohesion in member States.

Taking stock of the current, overall state of affairs in integration policies in the different member States, the report focuses on lessons learned since 1991 in fields such as diversity and cohesion, citizenship and participation, management of migratory movements or minority protection.

Forward-looking in its nature and taking into account "that peace, stability and harmonious relations between communities are not to be taken for granted, but require the unabated commitment of European governments and citizens to bring them about", it attempts to identify ways and means of establishing, with a comprehensive approach, positive community relations for European societies of the new millenium through the promotion of a political, economic, cultural and legal environment favourable to diversity and the promotion of social cohesion based on the strengthening and protection of human rights and fundamental freedoms, and particularly of social rights.

I warmly thank the author of the report, Mr Jan Niessen, Director of Migration Policy Group, and his team (especially Ms Lori Lindburg), the European Cultural Foundation for the financial contribution to the elaboration of the report and the members of the drafting Committee MG-ED for their valuable co-operation.

Walter Schwimmer
Secretary General of the Council of Europe

Chapter I: The unfinished agenda

Europe has always been a continent of diversity. Diversity is a fact of life in Europe, not only between states but also within countries, regions and cities and among their populations. Globalisation continues to feed this diversity and cultivates the seemingly contradictory emergence of a global culture and the assertion of territorial and group cultures. Sophisticated means of communication and transport increase the possibilities for human exchanges, involving a growing number of people. European countries and populations cherish their own identity, heritage, values, traditions, languages and ways of life, the cumulative products of centuries of human and cultural exchanges. Europe values its diversity.

Cultural pluralism needs to be firmly based on the respect of differences, which implies equality, tolerance and non-discrimination. The assertion of cultural identities, shared values and a common history foster the sense of belonging to a community, be it a majority or minority community, a region, nation, state or continent. Acceptance of diversity and the interaction between cultures foster harmonious relations between people, enrich their lives and provides them with creativity to respond to new challenges. It is not the denial, but rather, the recognition of differences that keeps a community together. Without a respect for differences communities may turn in on themselves, ultimately leading to their disintegration, decline or disappearance. It may also lead to an identity lose and provoke aggression towards others.

Europe's history shows two faces in terms of respect and disrespect of differences. Equality and non-discrimination are enshrined in national and international laws and are upheld in everyday life. Intolerance, on the other hand, has led and continues to lead to violations of these laws and oppression of those who are regarded as different. European co-operation and integration are interrupted by wars within and between states and violent conflicts among groups of people. If there is one thing that Europe's history demonstrates, it is that peace, stability and harmonious relations between communities are not to be taken for granted, but require the unabated commitment of European governments and citizens to bring them about.

Europe is inextricably linked to and characterised by the dynamics of global exchanges between people and cultures. Economic, political and cultural globalisation poses a challenge to Europe's traditional boundaries and frontiers. As the world economy becomes increasingly borderless, some governmental powers are shifting from the national level to regional and international levels. National cultures are supplemented by a global culture, regional and trans-frontier cultures, and the cultures of specific categories of people. International mobility of highly, semi- and unskilled workers, businesspersons, tourists and artists accompanies and reinforces globalisation. European governments must respond to these developments, just as Europe's inhabitants need new competences to cope with accelerating changes.

In a global society diversity is not a hindrance but rather a requisite for societal and personal development. Oppression or negligence of differences denies the identity of communities and may undermine the social and political fabric of countries. Social cohesion and commitment to participate in the life of the community are strengthened when differences are recognised and valued. Persons identify themselves as belonging to more than one community. Their identities are mutable and change according to what is required by the circumstances. Governmental policies can contribute to an environment that values diversity and thereby promotes cohesion. An integral part of these policies is the tackling of the negative consequences of globalisation, such as uneven distribution of economic, social and cultural goods within and between communities, and the marginalisation and social exclusion of certain groups within society.

This report aims to contribute to the adoption and implementation of such policies while focussing on two particular groups, namely immigrants and minorities. Cultural pluralism has developed over the centuries and immigrants and minorities have played their own part in that process. By adding to Europe's diversity they have enriched and continue to enrich European societies. In this respect Europe also reveals its double face. Many European countries have been successful in including immigrants and valuing their contribution to society. On the other hand, there are many examples of violations of the fundamental rights of immigrants, forced assimilation or segregation and involuntary return. Majority and minority populations have lived together harmoniously for centuries to their mutual and overall society's benefit, but there is also an equally long history of disrespect and oppression of minorities. The respect of human rights and the promotion of good relations between states and among communities continue to require the intervention of governments.

The report concentrates on that which immigrants and minorities have in common, namely a distinction from other groups in society in terms of ethnic and national origins, cultures, languages and religions. In other words, this report does not deal with the movement of immigrants and minorities, but rather, identifies and describes the necessary components of social cohesion policies that promote the inclusion into societies[1]. These policies should be based on the respect of the fundamental rights and dignity of immigrants

---

1. The management of international migratory movements is the subject of another report recently published by the Council of Europe.

and minorities. They should also take into consideration that these people represent a great diversity among themselves in terms of national origin and identity, ethnic and cultural background, religion and skin colour, just as women and men play similar, yet distinctive roles in the process of integration.

In policy and public debates immigrants and minorities are often depicted as groups that have and/or cause problems. Without denying that there are still many difficulties surrounding the inclusion of immigrants and minorities, this report intends to look more at how societies can learn to use and appreciate the contributions of these groups in responding to societies' overall challenges. It therefore highlights positive rather than negative developments related to the inclusion of immigrants and minorities. Inclusion is a two-way process of adaptation and adjustment on the part of immigrants and minorities and the larger society, thus requiring the active involvement of all stakeholders. Government and civil society have their distinct role to play in the opening up of society and mainstream institutions. States and their citizens may expect that immigrants and minorities actively commit themselves to become part of society and subscribe to its fundamental values.

In 1991, the Council of Europe published the report 'Community and ethnic relations in Europe'. The report reflected the work undertaken by the Council of Europe and many of its member states throughout the 1980s. During the 1990, the report inspired the policies of newer countries of immigration including those of the Council's new member states. The Council decided to commission a new report that would build on the previous work by applying the principles of community relations to countries with minorities and/or established immigrant populations. This new report aims to stimulate policy debates by analysing new developments, discerning new challenges and introducing new policy concepts. Such debates should underpin governmental policies and increase their acceptance among the population.

The climate in Europe has, in many respects, not improved with regard to relations between majority populations, immigrants and minorities. Immigrants and minorities are still frequently seen as competitors in the labour market, threats to cultural norms and national identities, and sources of a host of other societal ills. Ethnic conflicts and wars, ethnic cleansing, racist expression and violence, persisting patterns of direct and indirect discrimination, popularity of right-wing extremist and nationalistic politics, and the diminishing socio-economic position of significant numbers of immigrants and minorities relative to majority populations have posed some of the most blatant affronts to community relations policies. The new report aims to assist governments to better respond to these negative developments and offers recommendations for countering them.

The second chapter briefly reflects on what constitutes Europe and sketches major socio-economic, political and cultural trends. It assesses current migratory movements and immigrant and minority residents in Europe and defines the new challenges this presents. Chapter three summarises developments in the policy debates on the societal integration of immigrants and minorities. It explores new policy orientations describing and considers the policy implications of such policy concepts as diversity and cohesion, and citizenship and participation. Chapter four formulates strategic goals for member states of the Council of Europe and outlines a comprehensive approach to achieve these goals. The remainder of the report is devoted to policy implementation.

Chapter five demonstrates the importance of European co-operation and looks at the Council of Europe's legal instruments for policy areas explored in this report. Chapter six discusses the role of the various branches of government, governmental agencies and non-governmental actors. Chapter seven offers examples of governmental and non-governmental policies and practices concerning socio-economic inclusion, cultural diversity and political participation. This chapter draws from work undertaken by the Council of Europe during the last ten years, while considering recent practices within member states. The eighth chapter explores how the implementation of policies can be monitored and how to measure their results. Migration statistics and information on the state of ratification of European conventions can be found in the annexes of the report, as are relevant Council of Europe publications.

Although the report is the result of consultations within the Council of Europe and is addressed first and foremost to governments, the Council of Europe nevertheless hopes that it will also stimulates a wider debate on diversity and cohesion in Europe that engages both governmental and non-governmental actors. The report is not intended to provide all of the answers, but rather, to stimulate discussion on the value of diversity, what the limits of diversity might be, and how to strike an effective balance between promoting diversity and maintaining cohesion. This dialogue should include immigrants and minorities from the outset, as actors, and not only subjects, of these debates.

Chapter II: Global exchanges and new challenges for Europe

This chapter briefly reflects on what Europe stands for and sketches major socio-economic, political and cultural trends (2.1), characterises current migratory movements and immigrant and minority populations in Europe (2.2) and defines new challenges for Europe (2.3).

2.1 Stretching boundaries and accelerating changes

It is not always easy to determine precisely what constitutes Europe's frontiers. There are multiple meanings implied by the term "European" and to interpretations given as to what Europe stands for, both historically and in terms of values and cultures.

Part of a vast mainland, Europe is sometimes depicted as a Eurasian peninsula. Eastbound expansions extended Europe's frontiers into Siberia and Central Asia. The Atlantic Ocean forms one of Europe's frontiers, but where does that leave Iceland and Greenland? Moreover, could one not also argue that Europe has spread itself beyond this and across other oceans by creating European settlements and societies in the Americas, Australasia and Southern Africa? Yet another body of water has proven to be equally ineffective in separating Europe from neighbouring continents. The Mediterranean has been for centuries the highway for economic, cultural and human exchanges, producing the civilisations upon which Europe is built.

Given this context, it appears far less complicated to draw borders on a map and divide Europe into states distinct from other non-European states. Drawing maps, however, is a never-ending exercise. For centuries and even today, borders have shifted within and beyond Europe, particularly during an era when European empires encompassed territories on other continents.

Perhaps the most simple and pragmatic way to determine what constitutes Europe is through membership in European political institutions. Even this, however, poses some difficulties. The European Union unites fifteen European states. It formally associates itself, however, with extra-European former colonies and various types of overseas territories. The Council of Europe brings together forty-one European states, however, some of these are members of the Commonwealth of Independent States, which brings together European and Central-Asian states.

Europe's history is therefore one of stretching frontiers and global expansion, the shifting and lifting of borders, and the movements and settlements of people. This history complicates, yet significantly enriches the meaning of "European".

The roots of European civilisation are Graeco-Judaic, Roman and Byzantine Christian, North African and Ottoman Islamic. With the shifts of power centres from the Mediterranean to the Atlantic, Europe became a predominantly Christian continent. Through the age of Enlightenment and subsequent scientific, industrial and technological revolutions, a system of values evolved of which rationalism and secularism, individual freedom and solidarity, democracy, rule of law and human rights are the main components.

These developments laid the foundation of (mainly western) Europe's global economic and political power and its prominent role in the ages-old process of globalisation. The Christian faith became a world religion and European values acquired universal acceptance, later enshrined in international law. European languages such as English, French, Spanish and Portuguese became world languages and are spoken by a greater number of people outside as opposed to inside Europe.

Europe, however, has not always lived up to its own standards. In countries across Europe over the last hundred years, the establishment of left- and right- wing dictatorships has interrupted the process of democratisation. Cultural and ethnic intolerance has led and continues to lead to wars and the oppression of minority populations. Colonial dominance has violated human rights of colonised peoples and, in many instances, deprived them from their own identity.

No unified European culture has emerged in the course of history. On the contrary, Europe thrives on its diversity. The Christian tradition produced diverse denominations – Roman Catholic, Orthodox and Protestant. In certain parts of Europe, Islam remained the dominant faith. The Jewish Diaspora has lead to the establishment of Jewish communities in many European countries.

Linguistically, Europe is even more diverse and its linguistic map depicts numerous languages and dialects. They, in turn, form the vehicles of national, regional and local cultures, which become the expressions of national, regional and local identities.

Within nations and states, there are cultural differences between metropolitan, urban and rural areas. Geography is often used to demarcate different cultures, but social and economic position also distinguishes people culturally. Upper, middle and lower classes have their own distinct cultures. Just as there is a culture of the affluent, there is a culture of poverty. Each of these cultures are showing striking similarities beyond national borders and across Europe.

Another factor contributing to Europe's diversity is a certain degree of openness, which in the past accompanied Europe's colonial dominance, and which today still accompanies its global outreach. Encounters with and exchanges between people and other cultures lead to absorption of elements of these cultures into European cultures. This process is reinforced by the settlement of immigrants originating from other continents.

To summarise, Europe is inextricably linked to the dynamics of global exchanges between people and cultures. Traditionally, these exchanges have been of vital importance for Europe and they will remain essential for its further development.

Although the term globalisation is used to characterise this last part of the 20th century, the process of global outreach is more than five hundred years old. Throughout the ages, globalisation has kept pace with the means of transportation and communication.

With regard to Europe, sporadic and explorative expeditions led to the establishment of trade posts across the globe. Settlements became the basis of colonial rule or for the integration of non-European countries into European empires. With the end of the colonial and imperial era, the relations between the rulers and the ruled changed fundamentally, yet political and economic ties and human and cultural exchanges were in most cases maintained.

Knowledge of other countries and cultures has gradually increased and deepened and is experienced by a growing number of people. Such cultural exchanges occur through temporary migration and permanent settlement, global business transactions, international tourism, satellite communications and other medium.

Thus, while globalisation is not a new phenomenon, it is presently characterised by accelerating and intensifying global exchanges involving more people than ever before. These far-reaching socio-economic, political and cultural changes require adequate responses from governments and other stakeholders, in particular, when these changes lead to impoverishment and marginalisation of countries or groups of people within the population.

Socio-economic changes

With the end of the Second World War, western countries adopted programmes that aimed to liberalise trade and to gradually remove obstacles for the movement of capital, services, goods, information and persons. The implementation of these programmes necessitated intensive co-operation between countries, for which international institutions were created, such as the International Monetary Fund, the World Bank, the Organisation of Economic Co-operation and Development and the General Agreement on Trade and Tariffs (currently, the World Trade Organisation).

Liberalisation supported by the development of information, communications and transport technology, created new opportunities for companies to operate trans-nationally in an increasingly borderless economy. As a consequence, it has become more difficult to regulate such companies through state interventions and national laws, and many wield economic power that equals or surpasses that of individual states.

National economies are rapidly being integrated into the expanding world economy, a process that normally takes place through intensified regional co-operation. National economic and monetary policies are to a great extent subject to decisions taken at regional levels and are bound by international agreements such as the GATT and GATS.

West European countries are among the motors of the globalising economy. The European Union is establishing a common market and monetary union. It has established the European Economic Area (which includes all EU Member States and Liechtenstein, Iceland and Norway), begun negotiations with Central European countries on their future membership in the Union, and set the goal to establish a free trade zone in the Mediterranean basin.

Market economies have produced economic growth and raised the standard of living of entire populations. Through governmental interventions and co-operation between governments and their social partners, national income was more equally distributed and considerable investments were made in public services such as education and health.

The Soviet Union and the states of Central and Eastern Europe were not fully part of the process of economic globalisation, but created centralised economies, which mainly operated within their own internal market (The Comecon)[1]. The inefficiency and final collapse of those economies were one of the main reasons of the end of totalitarian regimes in central and Eastern Europe.

After the collapse of the system, former state-economies are being replaced by market economies, extending the impact of economic globalisation to the countries of the former Soviet Union. Most of the Central European countries are seeking membership in the European Union and some are already in the process of accession, adjusting their policies to those of the Union. The Russian Federation and other former Soviet Republics have re-grouped themselves and seek other economic alliances.

Although the current economic restructuring of West and East European countries have different origins and follow different courses, their economies are similarly plagued by high unemployment, job insecurity and social exclusion. Processes of fragmentation along economic lines are weakening social cohesion. Traditional remedies for solving these problems have been drawn

1. Soviet Union, Bulgaria, Hungary, Poland, Romania and Czechoslovakia.

into questions (the welfare state model), or no longer exist and are yet to be replaced by another system (the social contract model).

Countries across Europe face a similar set of challenges. Their inhabitants must acquire new competences to cope with economic transformation and the requirements of the new labour market. New ways of promoting solidarity between various groups in society are in need of development. The gap between those who profit from economic globalisation and those who do not – a divide within and between countries – needs to be bridged.

Political changes

The end of the divide between the West and East had considerable consequences for Europe's political order and for the co-operation between states. Economic globalisation requires that governments at all levels redefine their role and look for partnerships with non-governmental actors.

Some European states have (re-) gained their independence. Democratic governments are being formed and the development of civil society is being promoted. In some cases, new states have emerged on the basis of national or ethnic groupings.

In some parts of Europe, these changes are accompanied by violence and wars between ethnic groups and through ethnic cleansing. In other parts, they have lead to increased ethnic tensions within states or to tensions between states on issues related to the treatment of minorities.

Political and military alliances are shifting and co-operation between European states is undergoing fundamental change. During the Cold War, the Organisation for Security and Co-operation in Europe (OSCE) provided a unique platform for dialogue between the West and the East, *inter alia*, on issues of human exchanges and minorities. The OSCE is still playing an important role in these and other areas, such as conflict resolution and electoral monitoring in new democracies.

The Council of Europe, for long an alliance of Western countries, incorporated in very short period the countries of Eastern Europe. The Council has positioned itself as the platform for pan-European co-operation, notably in the fields of democracy, civil society and human rights, and co-operation on social and cultural matters. The Council is presently challenged to maintain its role as the guardian of European conventions, particularly those pertaining to human rights, and to convince all of its members that the protection of the human rights of individuals and minorities is a common and shared responsibility.

With the end of the Cold War, the North Atlantic Treaty Organisation (NATO) expanded its membership and has assumed new responsibilities, as is evident in its Balkan interventions.

The increasing interdependence of countries and continents calls for political co-operation on a global scale. The United Nations and its specialised agencies provide a platform for such co-operation. Meetings of the Group of Eight and the informal meetings of the World Economic Forum are further expressions of political globalisation.

In both West and East Europe, the role of the state is undergoing change. EU member states, by working together supra-nationally, have transferred some of their sovereignty to the Union's institutions. Although the goals of the Union are primarily economic and social, it is gradually assuming more responsibilities in other areas, such as the environment, culture and human rights. Moreover, the powers of the European Parliament are slowly being extended to the level of national parliaments. This supra-national co-operation is accompanied by a transfer of powers to regions and by co-operation between regions, either within or in more than one country.

In the former communist countries, the state is no longer controlled by one political party. In most of these countries the state is governed through parliamentary systems, and in some others through a presidential system. Successive elections have led to changing coalitions between political parties and to a system of power sharing between the various branches of governments. In addition, decentralisation, in varying degrees, has empowered provinces and regions. Co-operation between regions and across national borders is an important development in East Europe. The political instability accompanying these changes has in many countries, but not all, come to an end.

Civil society has often pressed for political change or has drawn governmental attention to issues in need of address. Governments have also begun to re-examine and modify their roles, leading to a greater openness to form partnerships with a variety of non-governmental actors. A pragmatic assessment of the limits of government in social and economic life has increased their willingness to enlist the support and advice of the business sector in designing strategies aimed at economic development and social inclusion.

Good governance, usually associated exclusively with governmental practice, is becoming a matter for governmental and non-governmental actors alike when they act in partnership. Several governments are recognising a need to relinquish some of their social responsibilities, while some businesses are assuming a greater social role. Civil society, when calling for respect of human rights, can find a powerful ally in the business sector, which can make implementation of these rights a condition for investment. Finally, the business sector profits from governmental investments in infrastructure, security, education and technological innovation.

Good governance poses a major political challenge for Europe. Against the backdrop of political change and its accompanying tensions and (armed) conflicts, a new balance must be struck between governmental interventions at the local, regional and international level, and between the policies and practices of governmental and non-governmental actors.

Cultural changes[1]

Globalisation, on the one hand, leads to a 'deterritorialised' or global culture and, on the other, to the assertion of territorial and group cultures. These dual responses are not necessarily contradictory, nor are they mutually exclusive. Culture provides individuals and communities with a common identity, and therefore, to a sense of belonging – in a deep and permanent way – to a group, a community, an ideal or an inspiration.

The developing global or cosmopolitan culture is based on universal values and absorbs regional particularisms. It stimulates the emergence of significant similarities in lifestyles, trends, entertainment and arts. Cosmopolitanism is loosing much of its elitist character as modern technology and sophisticated means of transport and communication make this type of culture accessible to a greater number of people.

Cultural diversity is a fact of life in Europe, not only between but also within countries. In democratic societies, a consensus is emerging that values cultural diversity and recognises the right to be different. Members of different cultures have their own traditions, heritages and views on the future. Cultural pluralism and interculturalism (the exchange and interaction between cultures) enrich life.

The assertion of particular identities is often a response against the homogenisation of cultures or a reaction to past or present repression of cultural differences. Whether this translates into antagonistic attitudes towards other cultures depends also on economic and political factors. Such attitudes can be witnessed in various parts of Europe and take the form of extremist nationalistic and xenophobic movements.

Where the impact of economic globalisation impoverishes specific groups, regions or countries, the assertion of cultural identity may serve as a means of mobilising against those who are seen to cause or profit from it. The alleged cultural superiority of a nation or an ethnic group may attempt to compensate for economic downturn and exclusion. Economic development and social inclusion strategies offer alternative instruments to excluded peoples and regions. In a global marketplace, cultural diversity is not a hindrance, but rather an asset to economic development.

When nations and regions with distinct cultural identities are not recognised, and their cultures repressed, the understandable call for recognition and

---

1. This section is, in part, inspired by *In from the margins. A contribution to the debate on culture and development in Europe* (Council of Europe, 1997).

more (cultural) autonomy can manifest as chauvinism and hostility towards other nations and regions. Cultural co-operation between states is therefore instrumental to promoting mutual respect and understanding.

The assertion of particular identities is not antagonistic or exclusive per se. It is more often a positive identification with a region, a country, or a continent, which is not detrimental to or disrespectful of others. Nor is it exclusive, since one can belong to a minority culture while feeling a part of the wider society of which a minority is part.

Increasingly, persons do not identify themselves as belonging exclusively to one group or another, to a minority or a majority, or to a particular political entity. Identities are mutable and change according to circumstances, and individual choice plays a great role in determining when one belongs to a particular group. A sense of being a part of a global culture might at other times be overtaken by a sense of sharing the particular values of a certain region or group.

The challenge is to avoid that cultural diversity and multiple affiliations lead to the denial or disrespect of universal and cross-cultural values that are vital for relations between individuals and groups of individuals within society.

2.2 Immigrants and minorities

In spite of the similarities and differences in immigrants' and minorities' backgrounds, both have significantly contributed to Europe's cultural, religious, linguistic and ethnic or racial diversity.

Migration and immigrants

Migration comprises an integral part of Europe's history and an important dimension of its current reality. There is not a single European country that has not been affected by migratory movements. European citizens have and continue to emigrate from and within Europe, while migrants and refugees from other parts of the world arrive to build new lives in a Europe.

Whereas immigration is part of the national identity and heritage of Australia, Canada and the United States, European countries consider themselves first and foremost as countries of emigration. What these continents nevertheless have in common is a significant governmental involvement in immigration matters. They have put in place procedures for admitting immigrants and refugees and programmes to facilitate their integration. This distinguishes them from other continents where governments play a far lesser role in these matters.

Many European countries have succeeded in integrating migrants and refugees. This is not to say that the integration process – often taking more than one generation – has met without conflict and tension between newcomers and groups within the host population. Nor does it ignore the fact that many of these migrants and refugees opted to return to their countries of origin.

International law makes a clear distinction between refugees and various categories of migrants. The 1951 Convention relating to the Status of Refugees established the definition of "refugee". The 1990 Convention on the Protection of All Migrant Workers and Members of their Family provides a universal definition of a "migrant worker" and of various categories of migrants (such as frontier workers, seasonal workers, itinerant workers, project-tied workers, self-employed workers, etc)[1].

While these or similar definitions retain their value and serve as a basis for migration and refugee policies in many countries, they do not always correspond to a complex and changing reality. A more recent addition to the policy and public debates, for instance, is the concept of *forced and voluntary migration*.

It is not always easy to determine what constitutes "forced migration", nor to distinguish whether a person is forced to leave one's country for political, socio-economic or other pressing and valid reasons. Forced migration can nevertheless be understood to refer to conditions, other than individual choice that induce migration. Although migration is almost always based on individual choices, options are substantially reduced when migration becomes a last resort and an indispensable part of survival strategies. While there are still significant numbers of persons who can be classified as "refugees" (in the 1951 Convention terms), "war refugees" or persons who migrate for (self-) employment reasons, an even greater number of persons are forced to leave their country because of a combination of factors. These factors may include extreme poverty and the lack of possibilities for a dignified life, social deprivation and collapse of the social fabric, political instability and collapse of the political fabric, brutal violations of human rights and dignity as well as generalised violence, ecological degradation and man-made natural disasters.

The mobility of labour and service providers is part and parcel of a globalising economy. Voluntary temporary and long-term migration takes different forms including high-skilled and less skilled labour migration, service providers and scientific exchanges.

Contrary to prevalent opinion, the principal migratory flows are not towards developed countries, but are essentially concentrated within developing countries. Current statistics estimate the number of people living outside the

---

1. The Convention on the Status of Refugees is, together with the Protocol, signed and ratified by a great number of European countries. On the contrary, the Convention on Migrants Rights has been signed by only one European state.

country of their birth to be 125 million. This figure corresponds to over two percent of the total world population. Fifty-two percent of these 125 million migrants are concentrated in developing countries; while developed countries take in only 56.7 million. The OECD reports a stabilisation in legal immigration flows to member countries over the last four years[1].

In all European countries, migrants constitute a diverse group, reflecting the complexity of global migratory movements. This includes established communities of immigrants, longer-term and temporary workers, frontier workers and merchants. Among them there are unskilled workers and highly educated people. Many immigrants have come from former colonies and the former non-European Soviet Republics. Refugees and war refugees constitute other groups. Still others are members of ethnic groups who have returned to the country of distant or recent origin (repatriates). Some are returning deportees. Undocumented or irregular migration also forms an important component of international migratory movements, further diversifying the group of migrants.

Migrant numbers are considerably less in the countries of Central and Eastern Europe than in Northern and Western European states. In the latter, established communities of immigrants of two and three generations live alongside significant newcomer populations. In Central Europe, many resident migrants view their stay as temporary, intending to migrate to Western Europe and North America (transit migration). The governments and publics of these countries similarly share the view of their countries as transit rather than permanent migration countries.

In contrast to Western Europe, the number of recognised refugees (according to the 1951 Convention) is also relatively small in Central and Eastern Europe. In those countries neighbouring countries in military conflict, the number of refugees granted temporary residence on humanitarian grounds is higher. In Eastern Europe, and in particular in the Russia Federation, there is also a significant number of internally displaced persons.

There are different groups among the population of repatriates. Some have returned after previous border changes or the creation of new states had placed them outside their national borders. In some countries, ethnic nationals of a very distant origin have "returned" after being granted favourable admission and assistance by governments. Others are returning deportees and their children, people who during a previous regime had been settled against their will somewhere outside their state.

---

1. UNDP, Programme of Action of the Cairo Conference, 5-13 September 1994; OECD, International migration trends, annual report 1996; John Salt, Current trends in international migration in Europe (Council of Europe, 1996). See for more statistical data Annex I.

Many countries that became independent in the early 1990s often include a number of stateless persons living on their territories who were former citizens of the now dissolved federal state. They can be considered as *"migrants sur place"* or stateless persons after having failed to apply for citizenship in the new state, or having been denied citizenship because of their ethnic origin. Family unification of these people has turned what used to be internal migration into international migration.

Historic and new minorities

Multi-ethnic and multi-national states and empires are a common phenomenon in Europe's distant and recent past, such as the older Ottoman and Habsburg empires and the more recent former Soviet Union. In these empires and in many of their successor states, minorities were and still are referred to as national minorities. In addition, smaller political entities can unite more than one nation, (as is the case of the United Kingdom and Spain), and many states have recognised minorities within their borders (such as, for example, Germany and Austria). Other groups that can be considered as historic minorities are the Roma, Sinti, Gypsies and Travellers, and such indigenous peoples as the Sami and Tatars. More recent migration has brought still more minorities to settle in West and East Europe.

Europe exhibits two faces when it comes to minority issues. There are many good examples of long periods of peaceful co-existence and interaction with minority inhabitants. International and national regimes provided protection of their rights, and national policies allowed for the maintenance of their culture and identity. There are also, however, many instances of conflict and war between the majority and minority populations and between various minority groups. Ethnic cleansing, population exchanges, pogroms and genocide are also a part of Europe's history.

There is no universally accepted legal definition of what constitutes a minority. At best, international organisations and various national governments have identified minorities by their ethnic, racial, linguistic or religious particularities. Usually the term refers to persons residing on the territory of a state who have historical and solid ties to that state, while possessing specific, ethnic, racial, religious or linguistic characteristics that they wish to preserve.

Most Central and Eastern European countries contain established minority communities. Their presence is often the result of earlier migratory movements, the emergence of states after the dissolution of multi-ethnic and multi-national empires, and/or the shifting of borders between states. The issue of minorities is closely linked with the formation of these nation states (in Central Europe and the Balkans), or to the status of political entities within the former Soviet Union (Union republics, autonomous republics, autonomous regions and autonomous areas).

Western Europe also has a history with minorities, although the issue is usually discussed and dealt with in other terms. Unlike Central and Eastern Europe, with its former multi-national empires, Western Europe has for centuries principally been comprised of nation-states. To preserve the unity of the nation-state, minorities were not afforded distinct recognition, but were considered equal citizens before the law, irrespective of their ethnic or national origins. The development of the nation-state went hand in hand with the development of liberal democracies and civil society.

Roma, Sinti, Gypsies and Travellers constitute particular groups of people totalling approximately nine million. These groups settle as larger or smaller communities in both West and East European countries. A number of them migrate within Central Europe, while others frequently move from Eastern to Western Europe. Statistics usually register them as citizens of the country they are coming from, raising considerable uncertainty about their national origin or nationality.

Indigenous peoples constitute a special group among the minorities. As is the case with minorities, there is no generally accepted definition of the term "indigenous peoples" in modern human rights law. In some countries terms such as Aboriginal peoples or First Nations are preferred. Two recent international human rights instruments, however, use the term indigenous peoples. The first is the 1989 International Labour Organisation's Convention on Indigenous and Tribal People and the second is the draft United Nations Declaration on the Rights of Indigenous Peoples. The use of the term indigenous peoples in these instruments presupposes the present-day co-existence of another ethnic group that is now dominant, either within the territory of the current state in question, or within an area traditionally inhabited by indigenous people. In other words, it is not sufficient that members of an ethnic group are descendants of the first known inhabitants of the state or area in question. There must be another ethnic group present and power relations involved before the descendants or the original inhabitants are understood as indigenous in the legal sense of the term. There are various indigenous peoples or people that claim such a status in Europe, for example, the Sami in Scandinavia and the Tatars in Russia and the Ukraine.

As a result of recent immigration, there are considerable numbers of immigrants of common background in many European countries. In some countries these groups are referred to as new, ethnic, racial or visible minorities.

Without loosing sight of the enormous diversity among these groups, this report refers to them collectively as minorities. What they share with each other, and with immigrants, is that they distinguish themselves from the majority or dominant groups in society in terms of ethnic or national origin, culture, language, religion and skin colour.

2.3 New challenges

Economic, political and cultural globalisation is posing new challenges to governments and societies at large. In this chapter, these challenges were described in terms of solidarity, good governance and multiple affiliations. In responding to these challenges, societies must also learn to use and appreciate the contributions of immigrants and minorities.

Solidarity within societies includes immigrant groups and minorities. Solidarity between countries includes tackling root causes of forced migration and offering (international) protection to minorities. Good governance entails empowering immigrants and minorities to address their specific problems and valuing their contributions in responding to society's overall challenges. Belonging to an immigrant or minority group merely adds another affiliation to the multiple affiliations these persons hold.

Immigrants and minorities do not often share a similar background. Historic minorities usually do not have a recent migratory history, but form long-established communities within states. They are thus able to claim recognition of their language, specific political representation and, in cases of indigenous populations, land rights. For those immigrants groups, who still feel a part of the culture of their country of origin, cultural and language matters are considered policy issues rather than granted rights. Immigrants seek participation in mainstream institutions and do not require specific political representation as exists for national minorities, nor do they have claims on land of the 'host country' as indigenous peoples may have.

Immigrants and minorities do have many things in common, however, and policies relating to them often concern similar issues. Minorities may have a migratory background, on one hand, while the violation of minority rights, on the other, may lead to migratory movements. They often share a distinction from other groups in society in terms of ethnic and national origins, cultures, languages, religions and skin colour. When addressing these issues, societies will have to respond to two challenges.

The first corresponds to immigration and the need to acknowledge that Europe has become a region of immigration. This involves an honest re-evaluation of Europe's history. Europe must consider itself historically as not only a region from which people migrated, but also as the final destination of many who have immigrated. This would do justice to immigrants groups throughout Europe, since the denial that Europe is an area of immigration essentially denies the existence of immigrants and the role they played and continue to play in Europe's history.

The second relates to minorities and the development of civil society. In a context of a developed civil society based on the principles of equality before law, there needs to be more openness for accommodating groups of individuals who define themselves as members of minority groups. In a context of multi-national and multi-ethnic states, application of the principles of civil society could contribute to easing ethnic tensions and conflict.

Chapter III: Policy developments and new orientations

This chapter summarises developments in the policy debates on the societal integration of immigrants and minorities (3.1) and explores new policy describing and reflecting on such policy concepts as diversity and cohesion, and citizenship and participation (3.2).

3.1 Societal integration and community relations

Migration and minority policies are designed and implemented in the context of socio-economic, political and cultural change, briefly summarised in the previous chapter. These changes result in highly complicated processes of societal disintegration and re-integration, affecting the lives of all persons, irrespective of national or ethnic origin. New political and personal attitudes are needed in order to establish "re-integrated" and cohesive societies that engage all of their inhabitants. Immigrants and minorities play an important part in this process, and may be better or lesser equipped than nationals to do so depending on circumstances. Moreover, the incorporation of immigrants and minorities into changing societies may be easier than their incorporation into societies that are more or less static.

The Council of Europe and many of its member states have adopted a basic philosophy for the integration of immigrants and the promotion of positive community relations[1]. First, it is recognised that governments – by adopting legislative and other policy measures in all areas of society – have a vital and active part to play in this process. Second, integration and community relations are not only matters for immigrants and minorities, but for society as a whole. Community relations refer to the whole range of challenges and opportunities resulting from the interaction between nationals and newcomers and between majority and minority groups. Integration involves not only adaptation by immigrants and minorities, but also the responses and adjustments of the society at large.

Migration and immigrant policies

In the first ten years after the Second World War, several countries across Europe were confronted with large influxes of refugees and returning nationals. Not long after, during the 1960s and '70s, North and West European countries began recruiting migrant workers, many of whom were joined by their families from the late 1970s and after. During the 1980s and

---

1. See *Community and ethnic relations in Europe. Final report of the Community Relations project of the Council of Europe* (Council of Europe, 1991).

1990s, these countries also received large numbers of refugees and asylum-seekers and, since the early 1990s, have begun to deal with the question of the temporary protection of refugees. Some have also begun (again) to recruit migrant workers on a temporary basis. These countries have gained considerable experience in the design and implementation of migration policies. In this report, these countries are referred to as older countries of immigration.

In other parts of Europe, countries have considerably less experience with immigration. Southern European countries and Finland and Ireland were, for a long period, sending countries and have only become receiving countries since the 1980s. Southern European countries form part of the Mediterranean basin that has its own tradition of human and cultural exchanges and migration dynamics. For many migrants Southern Europe is the gateway to Western Europe.

In Eastern and Central Europe, international (and in some cases, internal) mobility was restricted prior to the late 1980s, and few people were allowed to move abroad or within borders. In Eastern Europe, Soviet citizens moved between the Soviet Republics as part of the Soviet population policy. After the removal of the Iron Curtain, the end of the communist regimes in Central and Eastern Europe, and the break-up of the Soviet Union, international movements of people increased in almost all of these countries. In this report, these countries are referred to as newer countries of immigration. In varying degrees, they have begun to adopt legislation and other policy measures to address the issues of migration and the integration of refugees and immigrants[1].

Nowadays, migration ranks high on the political agenda of almost every European state, whether they are older or newer countries of immigration. Usually, a distinction is made between policies that aim to control or manage migratory movements and those that promote the integration of immigrants and refugees.

Governments of newer countries of immigration are recognising that many so-called "transit migrants" and other migrant and refugee groups will, in fact, remain in their countries. They have thus (in varying degrees over the last few years) begun to develop policy and other responses on integration and community relations alongside policies regulating the admission of returning nationals, immigrants and refugees. The development of integration policies is a part of, or profits from, changes in the countries' overall legal framework, including constitutional changes. Provisions outlawing

---

1. See, *Report of the Regional Conference to address the problems of refugees, displaced persons, other forms of involuntary displacement and returnees in the countries of the Commonwealth of Independent States and relevant neighbouring States* (UNHCR, IOM, OSCE, 1996).

discrimination on the basis of race and skin colour, national or ethnic origin, religion and belief are being inserted into national laws in many of these countries. Specific integration programmes are, if at all, primarily designed for returning nationals, deportees or refugees. Several countries are reviewing their existing legislation on nationality and citizenship, not only to respond to the immigration situation, but also to address the issue of national minorities and stateless persons. In some newly created states, the process of developing an independent citizenship policy is still underway and has not yet been finalised.

With few exceptions, older countries of immigration have never considered themselves to be countries of immigration, although they have, in fact, become de facto countries of immigration. Consequently, it has taken some time before governments began to address the issue of integrating immigrants into their receiving societies. In most of these countries, integration policies have been implemented and considerable experience gained as to how these policies work out in practice. In all of these countries, similar mechanisms have been adopted, including the securing of legal residence rights; measures to facilitate equal access to employment, housing, education and political decision-making; naturalisation and citizenship policies; and efforts to combat discrimination, racism and xenophobia[1].

Integration policies are often based on varying political philosophies and traditions in older immigration countries, with regular adaptations to respond to changing situations within their receiving societies. In spite of these differences, most of these countries are characterised by significant state intervention in establishing equal rights for long-term and legally resident non-citizens. Equal access to the institutions of the welfare state is viewed as key in integrating foreign-born populations. These policies are based on the notion of the equality of all individuals before law. Non-nationals should gradually acquire socio-economic and civil rights, while some rights would be exclusively reserved for citizens or nationals of the host society.

Some states went further and considered citizenship and naturalisation as central to the integration of immigrants and their families. Many adapted their laws on citizenship or nationality in order to facilitate naturalisation. Once they had acquired the citizenship or nationality of the host society, immigrants would automatically be granted the rights and obligations that come with that status.

Other countries went still further, believing that specific measures targeting (visible) minorities were needed in order to ensure these individuals' equal access to the major institutions of society. Such measures were intended to compensate for the fact that such persons usually come from disadvantaged

---

1. Migration Policy Group, *A review of the implementation of community relations policies* (Council of Europe, 1996).

positions (in terms of language ability, education, and job skills) and/or face social and structural impediments to their full participation in society in the form of racist or xenophobic discrimination.

In express policy terms, these variant approaches translate into the application of 'specific' or 'general' measures. Based on the desire to `level the playing field', specific measures target persons of immigrant or ethnic background in an effort to provide them with the skills and instruments needed to facilitate their integration into the host society. General measures, on the other hand, are directed towards society at large and involve an extension of those measures designed for national populations to immigrant and minority residents. Additionally, rather than targeting specific individuals, general measures seek to address problems affecting the entire society (i.e., housing, health care, etc.). In this way, it is intended that all social and economically disadvantaged persons be assisted, regardless of their ethnic or national background.

Varying trends in integration strategies may be viewed as an attempt by policymakers to achieve the right balance between general and specific measures. The more-or-less constant reformulation of this policy `mix' is often precipitated by major social and political upheavals. In this way, the current emphasis on general policies, particularly urban renewal measures, may be seen as a response to the growing popularity of extremist, anti-foreigner politics and incidents of urban unrest.

General policies also tend to be politically more palatable. In times of economic restructuring and high unemployment, immigrant labour is often viewed as competing with, or displacing, native labour. In such a climate, decision-makers do not wish to be seen as favouring immigrants and minorities over their national populations. In countries associated with more `ethnic specific' approaches, one can therefore see a general movement towards more general strategies over the last few years.

The movement towards general policies in some countries, however, has generated concern among immigrant and minority groups, as they stand to lose some of the protections they possess for facilitating their access to societal institutions. At a minimum, specific measures in the form of anti-discrimination legislation should accompany a more general integration approach. Others counter, however, that differential treatment on the basis of race and ethnicity only serves to highlight ethnic difference and to exacerbate anti-foreign sentiment.

Thus, the challenge for policy-makers continues to be how to balance interests and aims, general and specific measures, in the development of inclusion strategies. One answer may be found in what is referred to in some policy circles as 'mainstreaming' or, the desire to address the situations experienced largely by immigrant and minority groups across a broad policy spectrum.

Policy debates often focus on the problematic aspects of integration and on devising mechanisms to remove barriers to it. A new debate is emerging, however, that highlights the contribution of immigrants and minorities to society, and which values the fact that people are of different backgrounds and have multiple and diverse identities.

Minority policies

After the First World War, resulting in the dissolution of the Ottoman and Habsburg multi-national empires, emerging polities in Central Europe applied the principle of national self-determination and established new minority regimes, recognised under international law. State leaders concluded a series of international treaties offering protection to minority populations in their new states. In some instances, population exchanges took place.

The Second World War marked an end to the minority regimes in Central Europe, which were supplanted by the communist ideology of the unity of the workers' state. Minorities under this system were placed under tremendous pressure to adapt themselves to the dominant culture.

After 1989, national and ethnic identity again began to play an important role. National identity and the sense of belonging to an ethnic group or nation became, in some cases, the vehicle for the creation of new states or for reclaiming national independence.

The protection of minorities and the recognition of their rights thus re-emerged on the political agenda. Protection of minority rights became one of the conditions of membership of the Council of Europe. Similarly, the European Union made the establishment of relations between the Union and new independent states dependent on the protection of minorities. States whose nationals or groups of persons belonging to an ethnic group and who are also living in a neighbouring state or states have equally pressed for international and national legislation to protect minorities.

In some countries, settled minority communities are the second- or third-generation descendants of earlier migrants. Some established minorities are not certain how to relate to newly arrived refugees or immigrants from countries of their (distant) origin. In some instances, newcomers are welcomed into the minority communities; in others, they face reluctance and even rejection.

Under the Soviet Union, the variety of nationalities and ethnic groups did not pose an official issue. Social position, rather national or ethnic belonging, underpinned Soviet internal and external policies. Nevertheless, political pragmatism led to the recognition of national and ethnic differences between and within the Soviet republics, resulting in a system of ethnically based administrative/political units (union republics, autonomous republics, autonomous regions and autonomous areas). Power sharing and a sophisticated system of distributing economic benefits resulted, by and large, in co-existence among the almost 200 national and ethnic groups.

After the dissolution of the Soviet Union, the former Soviet republics gained political independence and began to receive their respective nationals who were living outside their new borders. Russians currently form the largest group among the repatriates, and there is strong debate within Russia as to whether Russian nationals should be encouraged to leave or stay in the former Soviet republics.

Historically grown attitudes and experiences of multiethnic, multi-religious and multilingual co-existence and conflict in Central and Eastern Europe influence present public perceptions and current understanding of cultural, religious and ethnic diversity. Some countries consider themselves to be multicultural because of the (in some cases, large numbers of) recognised ethnic, religious, lingual or cultural minorities who have been living in the territory for long periods. Other countries, although they were multicultural and multiethnic, did not recognise cultural diversity or ethnic minorities.

An assimilationist approach still predominates in most of these countries, requiring minorities (particularly Roma, gypsies and Travellers) and newcomers to prove their willingness to adopt local norms. Several minorities have challenged this situation, and their pressure (and that of international organisations) has led to the adoption of legal and other measures offering protection and/or official recognition. In some cases, minorities do not or are reluctant to exercise their rights or to benefit from measures allowing them to maintain their own identities.

New constitutions in most Central European countries contain provisions recognising minorities, whether they are religious, linguistic, ethnic or cultural minorities. Usually, the principle of equality before law is established. Some states have gone further by granting specific rights allowing minorities to preserve their identities. This includes: the right of mother-tongue education for children (in addition to compulsory teaching in the official language), the right to use the minority language in relations with the government and governmental services, the right to receive and send information in the native language, the use of the names and surnames in the minority language, the right to preserve the minority culture and to practise their religion, the right of association, etc.

Structures for dialogue between minority groups, and between minority groups and governments, have been set up in many of these countries. In some countries, minorities are entitled to official political representation and self-administration. In Hungary, Poland and Romania, constitutional provisions guarantee minority representation in the parliament (minority parties do not require as many votes as other parties to gain a seat in the parliament).

Minorities have the same rights in Lithuania as all citizens of the state. Minority parties are entitled to as many votes as other parties. Equality before the law is a recognised principle in the Republic of Lithuania. The rights belong to all individuals, irrespective of the race, colour, ethnic and national origin.

In the Slovak Republic, since November 1998, the state administration has created a structure to address the problems of minorities with their direct participation in decision-making processes. A Deputy Prime Minister for human rights, national minorities and regional development was appointed. The Government has set up the Council of the Government of the Slovak Republic for National Minorities and Ethnic Groups. Representatives of minorities have a decisive share in this council. The Parliament has established the Committee for Human Rights and National Minorities, within which a parliamentary commission for addressing the problems of Roma also operates. Since the early nineties, based on the results of parliamentary elections, the national minorities have had a permanent representation in the Parliament.

In Slovenia, representation in the National Assembly is guaranteed for important and long-standing minorities, such as the Italian and Hungarian minority groups. In Croatia, members of minority groups that constitute more than 8 percent of the total population are represented in the parliament and other government branches. Those minorities who make up less than 8 percent are entitled to elect five representatives for the Parliament's Chamber of Representatives. In Latvia, Lithuania and Romania, minorities form part of a national organisation that must be consulted in the decision-making process on matters affecting minorities. In Croatia and Hungary, self-administrative bodies at the national and local level have been established, which have the power of decision making on minority matters. In Estonia and Latvia, similar bodies have been created to deal with cultural matters. Sometimes minorities create such bodies themselves without official recognition, as is the case in the Ukraine and its autonomous republic of the Crimea. In this country the guaranteed representation in the national parliament has been abolished.[1]

In many of these countries, debates to review history are emerging, and new legislation offers the opportunity to create a climate that is favourable for the co-existence of ethnically diverse groups.

After the Second World War, Western European countries were determined to build democratic societies. European conventions were concluded which protected civil and political, as well as the social and economic, rights. These rights belonged to all individuals, irrespective of their race, colour, ethnic and

---

1. Overview of forms of participation of national minorities in decision-making processes in seventeen countries (Council of Europe/European Commission, 1998).

national origin. Those belonging to a minority group could also exercise these rights.

Such rights, however, were not always protected for or exercised equitably by minority groups. This has included religious minorities (such as those in Northern Ireland, Greece and Turkey), linguistic minorities (as in Belgium, Germany, Finland and Switzerland), indigenous people (such as the Sami in Scandinavia), and the Roma, Sinti and Gypsy and Travellers communities in many West European states.

In addition to the general policies of equality before law, West European governments have also made arrangements to accommodate the situation of specific minority groups. Austria has given special status to "Volksgrupen" (such as the Slovenians, Croats, Hungarians, Czechs, Slovakians and Roma and Sinti). In Germany, three national minority groups are officially recognised (the Sorben, the Danes and the Sinti and Roma). In Finland, Swedish speaking, Sami and Roma minorities have a special status under law. In Sweden and Norway, the Sami and other groups are recognised as minorities. Northern Ireland has specific legislation on religious discrimination. Moreover, in some countries, regions possess a certain degree of autonomy stemming from the specific history and particularities of the population, as is the case in Finland, Italy, Spain and the United Kingdom. Federal forms of government also grant "minorities" the right of self-government. This is the case, for example, in Belgium, Spain and Switzerland. These kinds of territorial arrangements are possible because these "minorities" are concentrated in certain regions.

As is the case in Central and Eastern Europe, the minority issue is back on the political agenda. This is due partly to the growing importance of regional governments and partly to the renewed determination to preserve regional or ethnic identities.

3.2 New policy orientations

Although not entirely new, the concepts of *diversity, cohesion, citizenship* and *participation* are increasingly being used, and are acquiring new meanings, in policy debates at the national and international levels.

Diversity and cohesion

Diversity is a concept of increasing usage in Europe, both in a descriptive and prescriptive sense. Equality forms the cornerstone of integration policies and minority protection (all people are equal and have equal rights). The concept of diversity has been introduced in the integration debates as a means of responding better to current demographic realities and as a process from which increasingly plural societies may benefit (all people are different and have a right to be different).

In the 1980s, the term was used primarily in the context of some country debates on multiculturalism and multicultural societies. Multiculturalism was used as a descriptive term (societies are multicultural) or as a prescriptive concept (societies should become multicultural societies). It was almost always associated with the presence of groups of people with different ethnic and racial backgrounds (national minorities, immigrants, Roma and gypsies) and not with the 'traditional' cultural diversity, for instance, between regions, urban and rural areas, professional categories, religions, etc.

Those who promote multiculturalism have called for equal treatment and acceptance of the cultural differences of immigrants, national minorities and Roma and gypsy populations. Among the opponents of multiculturalism are those who argue that the official recognition and promotion of multiculturalism undermines the unity of the state and could lead to the fragmentation of society. Other opponents go so far as to deny the equal rights and acceptance of these groups by defending the 'national culture and heritage'.

More recently, the term diversity has been used to address the variety of values, life-styles, cultures, religions and languages that characterise societies. First, the term refers to the diversity of culture, in general, and not exclusively as the by-product of migratory movements and settled minority communities. Secondly, when the term is applied to immigrants and minorities, it emphasises the value and not the problems associated with being different. Third, diversity recognises the simultaneous processes of cultural homogenisation (a global culture) and diversification (national and local cultures). Fourth, it stresses the fact that people usually (and increasingly) possess multiple identities, group memberships and cultural affiliations. Fifth, diversity is about voluntary and less about prescribed affiliations. Sixth, diversity deals in a creative way with the dichotomy of universal and particular values and culture. Finally, common values shared by civil society underpin the concept of diverse societies.

The term *cohesion* is most often used in the context of policy debates on employment and poverty. Measures are taken to reverse or remedy processes of (partial) societal dis-integration and the social exclusion and marginalisation of certain groups. These measures include: promoting and upholding the possession of fundamental social rights, the offer of certain social protections, access to housing for all, catering to the specific needs of certain groups at risk, opening up the labour market through education, training and life-long learning and institutional co-ordination[1]. Social cohesion policies aim to counterbalance the processes of societal fragmentation.

There are limits to the capability of states and societies to cope with diversity. Policies must therefore strike an effective balance between promoting

---

1. European Committee for Social Cohesion: Preliminary Proposals for a Strategy for Social Cohesion (CDCS 98) 8 – Appendix VI.

diversity and maintaining cohesion. Acceptance of diversity and interaction between cultures foster harmonious relations between people. In other words, cohesion can be promoted when diversity is valued.

Citizenship and participation

Most West European countries do not make a distinction between nationality and citizenship, and often use the terms interchangeably. Persons who have the nationality or citizenship of a state are considered to be full citizens of that state. Nationality or citizenship can be acquired on the basis of a short or longer period of residence.

The situation in many Central and Eastern Europe countries was and continues to be different. Persons may consider themselves as belonging to a nation or ethnic group (neither of which necessarily correspond with one state) while holding the citizenship of the state in which they are residing. Citizenship is essentially a contract between the state and its individual citizens. Nationality is a sense of belonging to a nation. To acquire citizenship of a state is therefore easier than becoming a national of a nation.

Nationality or citizenship, in the legal sense, entitles the bearers to full citizens' rights and guarantees de jure participation in the political and civil, social and economic and cultural life of the country concerned. Those who do not possess the nationality or citizenship of a state are excluded from a number of these rights (usually certain civil and political rights and the right to perform certain professions).

The European Convention on Nationality introduces one word – *nationality* – which it defines as the legal bond between a person and a state, regardless of a person's ethnic origin (Article 2). Consequently, citizenship could be used to define a different type of relationship between individuals or groups and political entities. Under this definition, citizenship could refer to the participation in civil society of all persons legally residing in a state, irrespective of their nationality and national and ethnic origin. As such, non-nationals would be gradually entitled to rights currently and exclusively reserved for nationals of the state.

The term citizenship does not exclusively apply to persons. It is increasingly used by governments (global citizenship of states) or businesses (corporate citizenship). Nor is citizenship exclusively linked to a state (trans-national citizenship). The introduction by the European Union of European citizenship for nationals of its Member States is one example. This does not replace the nationality of a Member State, but grants its bearers some additional rights. Finally, in a non-legal sense, people at times define themselves as local, national and global citizens (plural citizenship).

Participation in civil society is not only a right but also an obligation. Citizens ought to respect the laws of the country and subscribe to the society's fundamental values. They also ought to participate in elections or other decision-making mechanisms and they ought to respect the law and subscribe to societies fundamental values.

In short, a new concept of citizenship is emerging that allows for multiple and different types of affiliations. Citizenship means membership in civil society, entailing certain rights and obligations. It can therefore constitute a sense of belonging to more than one political entity (from local to global). This concept of citizenship is gaining further terrain in Europe.

Chapter IV: Strategic goals and comprehensive approaches

As explained in the first chapter, economic, political and cultural globalisation is posing new challenges to governments and societies at large. These challenges were described in terms of solidarity, good governance and multiple affiliations. Solidarity within societies includes immigrant groups and minorities. Solidarity between countries includes tackling root causes of forced migration and offering (international) protection to minorities. Good governance entails empowering immigrants and minorities to address their specific problems and valuing their contributions in responding to society's overall challenges. Belonging to an immigrant or minority group adds another affiliation to the multiple affiliations persons hold. In second chapter the concepts of diversity, cohesion, citizenship and participation were described. Although these concepts are not entirely new, they acquire new meanings in policy debates at the national and international levels.

The strategic goals of member states of the Council of Europe can now be described in terms of promoting cohesion by valuing diversity. They include:

- Implementing international human rights standards;

- Developing economic, social and cultural policies which are inclusive;

- Establishing equal treatment of all citizens irrespective of their social, national and ethnic origin;

- Elimination of legal and other barriers for the full participation of immigrants and minorities in all sectors of society;

- Combating all forms of discrimination on any ground such as gender, race, colour, language, religion, political or other opinion, national or social origin, association with a national minority, property, birth or other status;

- Making the (local) population more open for and tolerant towards immigrants and minorities;

- Valuing the diversity of the population in terms of personal abilities and assets, cultural background, linguistic skills and ethnic and national origin;

- Designing and implementing methods for inter-cultural exchanges and co-operation;

- Responding to the needs of a diverse population in terms of education, health, housing and other services;

- Fostering a sense of belonging and commitment to the state that reconciles multiple and varying affiliations people hold.

Policies to achieve these goals include the mainstreaming of immigrant and minority policies, the management of migration and the inclusion of immigrant and minority issues in international relations. Such policies require the recognition of the great diversity among the immigrant and minority populations and the targeting of specific groups among them, such as women and youngster.

Immigrant and minority policies benefit also greatly from co-ordination among governmental ministries, co-operation between governmental agencies and non-governmental actors and co-operation and consultation at the international level.

Mainstreaming

Mainstreaming can be described as the incorporation of issues related to specific groups into all areas of governmental policies. It fits into the shift from specific to general policies that can be witnessed in many European states and it is not only being applied to immigrants and minorities but also to issues as gender and disability. Mainstreaming should be based on well-defined policy aims and targets, capacity building, regular policy reviews, and strong political support and that of the persons concerned.

In a diverse society governments can promote cohesion by aiming to serve its diverse population. Governments have to identify the varying needs of its diverse population and tailor their services in such a way that these needs are accommodated. Targets can be set providing clear guidelines as to what kind of services must be given to which groups within the population. A diverse population has also diverse potentialities. Governments can create such conditions that the variety of skills, business and employment opportunities, and the diversity of arts, entertainment, music, dance and sport contribute to a country's socio-economic and cultural well-being.

The various governmental ministries need to be given the necessary human and other resources to address immigrant and minority issues when they design and implement their policies. Ministries acquire the capacity to act effectively on immigrant and minority issues by, among other means, creating task forces, developing expertise, recruiting staff with an immigrant and minority background and co-operating with non-governmental actors. Through regular policy reviews governments assess the effectiveness of their policies and make the necessary adjustments. The review also includes the verification of the involvement of all relevant ministries in the mainstreaming process. Relevant ministries are the interior, justice, labour, education, culture and social affairs ministries, but also the economic affairs, science and technology and foreign affairs ministries.

Political support for diversity policies and the mainstreaming of immigrant and minority policy contributes greatly to their success. This support is necessary in order to keep the issues of immigrants and minorities on the agenda and to respond adequately to the articulated needs and demands of these communities. The confidence of these communities in government is enhanced when government's personnel is a true reflection of the diverse population.

Managing migration

Governments have taken many measures to regulate or manage migratory movements and a comprehensive migration policy aims to safeguard the interests of the state and to protect the rights of the people concerned[1]. There is a complex interrelationship between immigration and integration. Disorderly and sudden movements of people, irregular migration and trafficking in human beings pose governments for serious problems in terms of reception and integration. Shrinking public budgets and less charitable public opinion have made it difficult for governments to justify the admission of large numbers of immigrants and their equal access to the labour market and services of the welfare states. Consequently, integration policies are often premised on restricted immigration.

However, immigration control and the way it is carried out may also have negative effects on the societal integration of immigrants. The language authorities often use to defend restrictive policies (such as "stemming the flows") may give the impression that international migration is an evil and that immigrants are not welcome altogether. This does not foster among the legally residing immigrants a sense of belonging to the receiving society. Families and networks of immigrants play and important role in the process of societal integration of immigrants and extremely restrictive rules for family reunification may have a negative effect on their integration. Existing visa regimes often hamper family visits and the occasional returns of the immigrants to their country of origin. In some countries or group of countries, internal travel and freedom of settlement is considerably restricted. These measures have equally a negative effect on integration. Finally, the way immigration control is carried out impacts on integration. It often happens that border controls are not carried out in all correctness and respect of dignity of the persons concerned. At random identity checks in public places often target exclusively on persons with a different skin colour or on those who appear to be a foreigner. This seems to suggest that all immigrants and minorities do not belong in the country where they have settled or have lived for many generations.

Regulated immigration for (self-) employment and family reunion purposes provides a sound basis for the integration of immigrants. Clear immigration

---

1. For a migration management strategy, see the report of the Reflection Group on Managing Migration in the Wider Europe: *Towards a migration management strategy* (Council of Europe, 2000).

rules define who will qualify for immigration and the basis of which criteria. This is important for both the immigrant communities and the authorities dealing with integration matters. Quick, correct and considerate processing of immigration application reduces the often long waiting periods and limits arbitrariness. This fosters the confidence of the immigrants and the public in the authorities. Furthermore, clear immigration rules and their correct implementation may enhance political and public support for governmental policies on immigration and integration policies.

International relations

International treaties define the rights and obligations of migrants and minorities and of governments that have to deal with migration and minority issues. These treaties form an integral part of international human rights instruments that, to a certain extent, also govern international relations. Bilateral treaties between states lay out in more detail how these states intend to regulate migration or to protect minorities. Respect of human rights and the combat against racial discrimination enhances a country's standing in the world and promotes stable and peaceful relations between states. Multi-lateral and bilateral treaties may foster links between states and could have a positive impact on other domains of co-operation between them.

States with a diverse population can better meet the challenges of globalisation for a number of reasons. Countries with a diverse population are familiar with diverse cultures, languages and customs and they developed expertise and sensitivity to act in a multi-cultural environment. Through personal links immigrants have access to political, economic and cultural networks in their country of origin. This facilitates the opening of new markets, the introduction of new products, the exchange of art and literature and the acquirement of new skills.

Immigrants and minorities may also play an important role in the economic development of their country of origin or where minorities of the same ethnic origin live. First generation immigrants transfer considerable amounts of money to their families in the countries of origin. In 1989, the International Monetary Fund estimated that official transfers amounted to $65 billion. This figure already demonstrates the significance of financial transfers of migrants, yet even they are largely under-estimated as unofficial channels for capital transfers are mostly used by migrants. Transferred remittances are often for private ends but are also invested in education, agriculture and the creation of small business. Returning migrants with their acquired skills can also contribute to the development of their country of origin. As immigrants and subsequent generations become settled, their relationship with the country of origin undergoes changes. Remittances usually diminish and are terminated and also return migration comes to an end. However, immigrants and minorities may continue to be involved in the development of their country of origin or within which live minorities of the same ethnic origin. Among them are private investors, managers and other personnel of international corporations and staff working for governmental and non-governmental development agencies.

Chapter V: European co-operation and legal instruments

This chapter summarises the importance of intergovernmental co-operation within the framework of the Council of Europe and the European Union (5.1) and looks at the relevant legal instruments adopted by the Council of Europe (5.2)[1].

5.1 European co-operation

Political idealism and pragmatism underlie a long-standing tradition of inter-governmental co-operation on migration and minority protection in Europe. This co-operation furthers the goals of European integration and the commitment to human rights and democracy throughout the continent. Among the more practical reasons for co-operation is the recognition that many issues arising from international migratory movements and the protection of minorities necessitate collaborative responses. Governments, but also non-governmental actors, are aware that international co-operation may be beneficial to the further development of national policies on cohesion and diversity. First, international co-operation facilitates the systemic exchange of information on policy developments in countries that are designing and implementing policies on cohesion and diversity. Second. It provides a platform for exchanging successful and less successful practices and promotes the development of joint initiatives and new approaches to diversity. Third, it assists governments in keeping immigrant and minority issues on the national and international policy agendas, and in linking them with broader policies. The impact of global changes has underscored the need for international co-operation.

There exist significant differences between newer and older immigration countries in terms of policy development and implementation in the fields of integration and community relations as well as in the approaches taken. Therefore, newer as well as older countries of immigration would benefit from regular policy exchanges between those countries that are in a similar stage of policy development and implementation. There are also similarities in the situation of newer and older countries of immigration and this justifies European co-operation between newer and older immigration countries. Similarly, exchanges between countries with a longer and a shorter experience of dealing with minority issues may be beneficial for the parties concerned.

---

1. In Chapter VII, Council of Europe actions, other that its standard-setting activities, will be highlighted.

By adopting and monitoring the implementation of legal instruments the Council of Europe sets international human rights standards. The Council is a platform for policy development, policy exchanges and assistance. It promotes co-operation between national, regional and local governments and trans-frontier co-operation between local and regional authorities. Finally, the Council facilitates the dialogue between governments and non-governmental actors.

All fifteen member states and candidate member states of the European Union are also member of the Council of Europe. However, the two European organisations differ from each other in many respects. This is mainly due to the fact that the Union is a platform for both supra-national and intergovernmental co-operation. Its members have conferred significant powers to the European Union institutions to enact legislation in a variety of policy areas, including free movement and, after the entry into force of the Amsterdam Treaty, immigration, asylum and anti-racism.

The free movement of persons is one of the four freedoms to be established alongside freedom of movement for services, capital and goods. These freedoms belong to the range of instruments used to achieve the goals of the European Union. These goals are defined not only in economic, but also in social terms and apply to EU citizens and, inevitably, third-country nationals. The establishment of a common market and economic and monetary union go hand in hand with social protections, social cohesion and raising the standard of living and quality of life.

The meaning of free movement of persons under Community law differs considerably from the meaning it is given in human rights conventions. The latter refer to everyone's right to travel freely within countries and to leave and return to one's own country. For the European Union, free movement is the instrument to regulate migration and integration of first and foremost EU nationals moving from one member state to another. Free movement of workers, self-employed persons and providers/recipients of services is, to a great extent, secured within the Union. Legislative measures have been adopted in the fields of access to the labour market, residence rights, establishment and family reunification. Nationals of member states are granted the right to look for and accept offers of employment in a member state other than their own and, having taken up a gainful activity, to acquire the right to reside in that member state. Free movement includes also the prohibition of discrimination based on nationality for workers in member states in the areas of employment, remuneration and other conditions of work and employment, as well as one's entitlement to social and fiscal advantages. Legislative and other measures guarantee equality of treatment in housing conditions and entitlement to social security benefits to all workers who are nationals of a member state and their dependants, irrespective of the place of employment or residence. Furthermore, measures have been adopted to eliminate restrictions on employment of nationals in certain public sector positions in member states other than their own, such as commercial providers of services (public transport, distribution of gas and electricity); operational services in public health institutions; education; and scientific research.

In contrast, immigration from outside and movement of nationals form non-member states within the Union have long remained almost exclusively within the domain of the individual member states. Equally, the integration of nationals of non-member states is primarily regulated by national laws and policies and by bilateral agreements between receiving and sending countries. However, Association and Co-operation Agreements concluded with third countries on the one hand (such as with Turkey, the Maghreb countries and countries in Central and Eastern Europe), and the implementation of Community social policies, on the other, have to some extent shaped national policies of non-discrimination and equal treatment. The Amsterdam Treaty, entered into force in 1999, is fundamentally changing this situation. Powers have conferred upon the institutions of the European Union to take legal and other measures on such issues as the lawful status of legal immigrants, condition of entry and residence of non-EU nationals and the free movement of these persons. In addition, the Amsterdam Treaty contains an anti-discrimination article enabling the Union to take legal and other measures against discrimination on grounds of racial or ethnic origin and religion and belief.

Whereas the Council of Europe and the European Union share common values and are committed to upholding human rights, including those of immigrants and minorities, EU policies in the field of migration and immigrant integration are an integral part of the establishment of the common market. This fact and the supra-national character of the Union distinguish the Union from the Council of Europe. Consequently, immigrant and minority policies of these organisations have a partly shared and partly distinct background, are adopted on the basis of different political procedures and have a different legal status.

5.2 Legal instruments and national policies[1]

Council of Europe conventions reflect the values and practices of its member states. On the other hand, these instruments inspire, influence and reinforce national policies. European conventions establish minimum standards throughout Europe. Adhesion by member states make it more difficult for governments, even when they are under pressure nationally, to fall back on a position in which these minimum standards are not respected. As far as

---

1. This section is, in part, based upon: Migration Policy Group, *A review of the implementation of community relations policies* (Council of Europe, 1996).

immigrants and minorities are concerned, national policies and European legal instruments cover four areas, namely securing residence rights, ensuring equal treatment, naturalisation and combating racial and ethnic discrimination[1].

A distinction can be made between policies needed for the admission, reception and residence of newly arriving immigrants, for the promotion of equal opportunities for long-term immigrants and minorities, and for societies with an ethnically, racially and culturally divers population. These distinctions correspond, to some extent, with the various stages of policy formation. Policies in newer immigration countries concentrate on issues related to entry and residence conditions and recruitment and reception, soon followed by measures promoting equal treatment with regard to working and living conditions. In a next stage policies are based on the recognition that immigrants are to stay in the host countries requiring the gradual extension of equal treatment to all spheres of life and the adoption of anti-discrimination legislation. Countries with established immigrants (second and subsequent generations) and countries with a minority population strive at finding a balance between specific and general approaches. Policies are designed to serve a diverse population and specific needs of certain groups are addressed. These countries may also have to deal with newcomers and adopt for this group adequate policies[2].

Securing residence rights

The securing of residence rights through the adoption of legislation is an important strategy for integrating immigrants and minorities. A legal framework provides much-needed clarity of the rights and obligations of the society and the immigrants or minority population. Without security, a person will not feel part of society and has little incentive to become part of it. Public authorities have little incentive to include immigrants and minorities with uncertain legal status in social and educational programmes. Temporary status also reduces employability and restricts immigrants and minorities to temporary and low skilled work. The establishment of normal family life is essential for immigrants and minorities to settle. Protection against expulsion enhances security and consequently integration.

There are a number of European Conventions that are important for securing residence rights. They include the Convention on the Protection of Human Rights and Fundamental Freedoms, the Convention on Establishment, the European Social Charter and the Convention on the Legal Status of Migrant Workers. They deal with such issues as admission, residence, employment, family reunion and expulsion.

---

1. For the state of ratification, see Annex II.
2. See for an elaborated check-list of policies for the various stages, Mary Coussey, *Framework of integration policies* (Council of Europe, 2000).

The Convention on the Legal Status of Migrant Workers deals extensively with recruitment (medical examination, vocational tests, work contract, entry and exit, adequate information, etc.). This Convention and the Convention on Establishment deal with matters related to entry and residence. According to the Convention on Establishment the contracting party shall facilitate the entry into its territory by nationals of the other parties for the purpose of temporary visits and shall permit them to travel freely within their territory. The contracting parties shall facilitate the prolonged or permanent residence in its territory of nationals of other contracting parties. Nationals of any contracting party lawfully residing in the territory of any other contracting party shall be authorised to take up a gainful activity on an equal footing with nationals of the latter party, provided they comply with one of the following conditions. First, they have been lawfully engaged in a gainful activity in that territory for an uninterrupted period of five years. Second, they have lawfully resided in that territory for an uninterrupted period of ten years. Third, they have been admitted to permanent residence. The two Conventions and the Social Charter establish the principle of equal treatment or no less favourable treatment of migrant workers with nationals with regards to working conditions and remuneration, housing and vocational training.

The Social Charter and the Convention on the Legal Status of Migrants contain provisions on family reunion[1]. According to the latter Convention, the spouse of a migrant worker who is lawfully employed and the unmarried and dependent children, as long as they are considered to be minors by the relevant law of the receiving state, are entitled to family reunion. The condition is that the migrant worker has housing available for his family and which is considered as normal for national workers. Another condition is steady resources sufficient to meet the needs of the family. A waiting period shall not exceed twelve months. It is noteworthy that the Social Charter mentions the age of 21 for the dependent children. However, this provision is interpreted as meaning dependent children for as long as they have not yet reached the age of adulthood.

The entry permission can be refused and residence permits may be withdrawn for reasons of national security, public policy or morals and public health. According to the Convention on the Legal Status of Migrant Workers unemployed migrants are allowed to remain in the receiving country when they are temporarily incapable of work as a result of illness or accident or because they are involuntarily unemployed. The Human Rights Convention provides some protection against expulsion where it recognises the right of private and family life of everyone under the jurisdiction of the state[2]. This

---

1. See also the International Convention on the Right of the Child (Article 10).
2. See also the International Convention on the Right of the Child (Article 9).

provision and rulings of the European Court of Human Rights make expulsion contrary to the protection of private and family life. The fourth Protocol to the Convention prohibits collective expulsion of aliens as well as the expulsion of nationals from their own state. The seventh Protocol prohibits expulsion of an alien lawfully resident in a state except when a decision to that effect is taken in accordance with law. The person concerned is entitled to submit reasons against the expulsion, have the case reviewed and be represented for these purposes before a competent authority.

A number of the above-mentioned European Conventions, but also the European Cultural Convention, recognise the right of finding employment in a state other than one's own and of travel and exchanges between states of students, scientists, artists and other persons. States are encouraged to facilitate mobility between states by avoiding cumbersome and costly procedures. The Framework Convention for the Protection of National Minorities encourages trans-frontier co-operation between local and regional authorities.

Policies in the member states are, to a greater or lesser extent, based on European conventions. Countries with a longer experience in dealing with immigrants have reviewed and adapted their aliens' laws, usually in correlation with these countries' recognition that temporary migrants had become immigrants. The establishment of permanent residence status provides for residence security, protection against expulsion and involves in some cases the merging of previously separate work and residence permits into one document. There is some erosion of the right of family life as a result of the introduction of restrictive measures (including lowering of age of children). There is also an increasing number of cases before the European Court on Human Rights on the expulsion of second-generation immigrants (double jeopardy). The newer countries of immigration are still in various stages of establishing criteria for granting legal residence. In some countries the situation of irregular migrants have been regularised. In other countries new legislation is adopted dealing with asylum procedures and residence rights of refugees and migrants.

There are significant differences between member states in terms of securing residence rights. In many member states national legislation offer more protection than required by the minimum standards of the European Conventions. In a significant number of member states the level of protection is below international standards. Therefore, member states are encouraged to sign, ratify and implement all the relevant instruments, in particular the Convention on Establishment and the Convention on the Legal Status of Migrant Workers. Member states may also need to look at their migration management and visa policies in order to see whether these policies have a detrimental effect on the promotion of (labour and scientific) mobility and human exchanges.

Equal treatment

In Europe equal treatment is the cornerstone of integration and community relations policies. It provides immigrants and minorities with equal opportunities and equal access to the labour market, education, health and other services. Equal treatment is seen as a major instrument to bring about justice and to promote solidarity among various groups in society. Legal and other measures to promote equality enable immigrants and minorities to participate fully in a society's economic, social and cultural life. On the other hand, these measures enable societies to benefit from the participation of a diverse population.

Equal treatment is firmly enshrined in European legislation. The European Convention on Human Rights and Fundamental Freedoms protects civil and political rights of everyone under the jurisdiction of a state. The Convention on the Participation of Foreigners in Public Life at Local Level grants political rights to migrants. The European Social Charter and the European Convention on the Legal Status of Migrant Workers establish socio-economic equality. Immigrants are entitled to basic social economic rights and they acquire more rights on the basis of length of legal stay in a country. The Framework Convention for the Protection of National Minorities and the European Charter for Regional and Minority Languages safeguards cultural, educational and linguistic rights of minorities.

The Human Rights Convention states that states shall secure to everyone within their jurisdiction the rights and freedoms as listed in the Convention. They include: the right to life, prohibition of torture or degrading treatment, the prohibition of slavery or servitude, forced or compulsory labour, the right to liberty and security of person, fair and public hearing in criminal cases, respect of private and family right, freedom of thought, conscience and religion, freedom of expression, freedom of peaceful assembly and association, and the right to marry. Some of these rights are repeated and elaborated on in the Framework Convention on the Protection of National Minorities. The Convention on the Participation of Foreigners in Public Life at Local Level grants lawfully resident foreigners the freedom of expression, assembly and association, provides for the establishment of consultative bodies to represent foreigners and entitles them to vote and stand for election in local authority elections.

The European Social Charter is the counterpart of the European Human Rights Convention in the sphere of economic and social rights. The Charter guarantees the enjoyment, without discrimination, of the following fundamental rights: the right to work, the right to just conditions of work, the right to safe and healthy working conditions, the right to fair remuneration, the right to organise, the right to bargain collectively, the right of children and young persons to protection, the right of employed women to protection, the right to vocational guidance and training, the right of protection of health and social security, the right to social and medical assistance, the right to benefit from social welfare services, the right of physically or mentally disabled persons to vocational training, rehabilitation and social resettlement, the right of the family to social, legal and economic protection, the right of mothers and children to social and economic protection, the right to engage in a gainful occupation in the territory of other contracting parties and the right of migrant workers and their families to protection and assistance. Migrant workers are entitled to a great many of these rights. In the Convention on the Legal Status of Migrant Workers these rights are more precisely described. With regard to social security, the European Convention on Social Security provides for equal treatment of nationals of contracting parties moving within the territory of other contracting parties, refugees and stateless persons. The Social and Medical Assistance Convention provides for equal treatment of nationals of contracting parties and refugees.

The ILO Convention on Migrant Workers (Supplementary Provisions) and the UN Convention on the Protection of the Rights of All Migrant Workers and Members of their Families deal extensively with the position of irregular or undocumented migrants. Both instruments protect basic human rights of all migrant workers.

The Framework Convention for the Protection of National Minorities recognises the right of persons belonging to national minorities to maintain and develop their culture and to preserve the essential elements of their identity, namely religion, language, traditions and cultural heritage. Governments shall encourage a spirit of tolerance and intercultural dialogue and take effective measures to promote mutual respect, understanding and co-operation among all persons living in their territory, irrespective of those persons' ethnic, cultural, linguistic or religious identity, in particular in the fields of education, culture and the media. The Framework Convention make many cross references to the Human Rights Convention making rights enshrined in the latter Convention more specific and applicable to national minorities. The Charter for Regional or Minority Languages calls upon the contracting parties to respect and promote regional and minority languages (languages of immigrants are excluded form this Charter). Contracting parties shall undertake to eliminate any unjustified distinction, exclusion, restriction or preference relating to the use of a regional or minority language and intended to discourage or endanger the maintenance or development of it.

In international law[1] and in many of the above mentioned European Conventions the principle is accepted that, in order to bring about equal treatment for all, special measures for specific disadvantaged groups may be

---

1. For example, the International Convention on the Elimination of All Forms of Racial Discrimination (Article 1) and the ILO Convention on Discrimination (Employment and Occupation) (Article 5).

taken for a limited period of time (positive action). This principle is also accepted and applied at the national levels, although it is from time to time challenged. Positive action can only be effective when immigrants and minorities are committed to participate in society.

It is not easy to make an assessment of the effectiveness of governmental policies in the field of promoting equal treatment of immigrants and minorities. There are a good many examples of successful policies from which benefit immigrants and national minorities. Voting rights for immigrants and special arrangements to guarantee political participation have been introduced in many member states. Some immigrant and minority groups operate extremely well in the labour market or as ethnic entrepreneurs. The recognition of minority languages and cultures has lead to the increase of the quality of life and has enriched societies tremendously.

On the other hand, statistical and other evidence show that in a significant number of countries there is a steadily deteriorating position of immigrants compared to that of national populations in areas as employment, housing and education. This is true not only of recent arrivals but also of newer generations born in the receiving countries. In some member states national minorities are still deprived of their fundamental rights or suffer from the lack of adequate policies. This contributes to their marginalisation. This situation calls for governments to re-orient and step up their equal treatment policies. It also calls for the ratification of the relevant European Conventions and a programme of assistance to and co-operation between member states on the implementation of the Conventions.

Nationality

Acquiring the nationality of the country of residence is a means of facilitating integration. Naturalisation secures, for once and for all, the legal status of immigrants and establishes complete equality before the law. Equally important is that naturalisation facilitates the development of a sense of belonging to the state and to society.

The European Convention on the reduction of Cases of Multiple Nationality and Military Obligations in Cases of Multiple Nationality, adopted in the early sixties, reflects the then prevalent interest of most member states to reduce the number of cases of multiple nationalities. The position of many member states has changed as a result of the increased mobility and the settlement of immigrants. Consequently, a Protocol was adopted allowing dual nationality for, among other persons, children of immigrants.

Coinciding with political changes in Central and Eastern Europe, the Council of Europe adopted the Convention on Nationality. This instrument must avoid as far as possible statelessness and discrimination in matters related to nationality. The Convention recognises the right of the state to determine under its own law who are its nationals and everyone's right to have a nationality. The rules of the state on nationality shall not contain distinctions or include any practice which amount to discrimination on the grounds of sex, religion, race, colour or national or ethnic origin. The Convention sets out clear rules regarding the procedures of applying for nationality (reasonable costs and delays, right of judicial review, etc.). Children having different nationalities acquired automatically at birth shall retain these nationalities. When nationality is acquired by marriage, spouses shall retain the nationality they already possessed.

In cases of state succession, contracting parties concerned shall regulate nationality matters by agreements among themselves, while respecting the rights and obligations included in the Convention. In deciding on the granting or retention of nationality in cases of state succession, each contracting party shall take account of the genuine and effective link of the persons with the state, their habitual residence, their will and their territorial origin.

In older countries of immigration naturalisation legislation has been adapted in order to facilitate the integration of immigrants. With a few exceptions, naturalisation procedures have been eased. Increasingly the question of naturalisation has come to hinge on questions of dual nationality, which in some countries is allowed and in others not. There is an emerging desire to make the acquisition of nationality something more than merely an administrative act and to organise, for example, a ceremonial event around it. Such an event should emphasise the immigrants' commitment to participate in society and society's commitment to value this participation. Newer countries of immigration begin to revise their nationality legislation as well.

Nationality legislation is also undergoing changes in countries with a significant minority population. Newly created states or states which have regained their independence are putting in place national legislation. New independent states born out of a federation of states often adopted simple procedures for the acquisition of nationality within the first years of the creation of these states. It turned out that not all persons entitled to nationality could acquire it within the set time limits. In other states nationality legislation has a discriminatory effect making it difficult for some minorities to acquire the nationality.

The Convention on Nationality is a useful instrument to shape national policies on nationality. The Council of Europe can assist member states to implement the Convention and to solve a number of problems related to the acquisition of nationality by immigrants and minorities.

Combating racial and ethnic discrimination

Racial and ethnic discrimination undermines the basis of democratic societies and is a direct violation of the fundamental rights of its victims. Immigrants and minorities are among the victims and they suffer from various forms of discrimination: from open or direct discrimination to indirect or institutional racism; from racial violence or harassment to inferior or degrading treatment. This not only prevents immigrants and minorities to participate fully and on equal basis in society, but also deprives society from the benefits of the skills and capacities of its entire population. Moreover, racism destroys the relationship between various groups in society and has the capacity to destabilise a country. The way immigrants and minorities are treated and discrimination is combated influence the relationships between states.

The most forceful international legal instrument against racism is the International Convention on the Elimination of all Forms of Racial Discrimination. This Convention has influenced the national anti-discrimination policies of many European ratifying states. As far as European Conventions are concerned, many of them contain provisions that the rights enumerated in that convention shall be enjoyed without discrimination on various grounds including race and ethnicity. The relevant clause in the Human Rights Convention is the most extensive in terms of grounds of discrimination. It states that the enjoyment of the rights and freedoms set forth in this Convention shall be secured without discrimination on any ground such as sex, race, colour, language, religion, political or other opinion, national or social origin, association with a national minority, property, birth or other status. In terms of enforcement the Human Rights Convention is the strongest Convention. Everyone under the jurisdiction of a state is entitled to the rights and freedoms listed in the Convention. Any person, non-governmental organisation or group of individuals claiming to be victim of a violation by a contracting party of the rights enumerated in the Convention, may address petitions to the European Court of Human Rights after national remedies have been exhausted. The rulings of the Court are binding. All member states are party to the Convention.

Compared with other international instruments, the protection provided by the Human Rights Convention is limited because its anti-discrimination clause is not an independent prohibition of discrimination. It prohibits discrimination only with regard to the rights and freedoms set forth in the Convention. A Protocol to the Convention can provide further guarantees in the field of equality and anti-discrimination. A draft of such a Protocol is pending adoption by the Committee of Ministers. The draft contains a general prohibition of discrimination. It states that the enjoyment of any right set forth by law be secured without discrimination on ground as sex, race, colour, language, religion, political or other opinion, national or social origin, association with a national minority, property, birth or other status. No one shall be discriminated against by any public authority on any of the above-mentioned grounds.

The climate in Europe has not improved – and in some instances has deteriorated – with respect to relations among host nationals, immigrants and minorities. Immigrants and minorities are still frequently seen as competitors in the labour market, threats to cultural norms and national identities, and sources of a host of other societal ills. Racist expression and violence, popularity of right-wing extremist politics, and the diminishing socio-economic position of significant numbers of immigrants and minorities compared to country nationals have posed some of the most blatant affronts to social cohesion policies. As a consequence, governmental and non-governmental actors have augmented their efforts to confront the persistence of racist and xenophobic attitudes. These have included, *inter alia*, the adoption, review and strengthening of anti-discrimination legislation and criminal codes, the establishment of voluntary codes of conduct, anti-racism demonstrations and campaigns, and inter-cultural curricula. Taken together, these measures are designed to protect the victims of discrimination and to promote more tolerant attitudes within society as a whole. These activities on the national level have been initiated or reinforced by international co-operation (for example, in the European Commission against Racism and Intolerance) and campaigns (for example, the All Different All Equal Campaign).

Chapter VI: Governmental and non-governmental actors

This chapter looks at the role of governments and governmental agencies in the promotion of diversity and cohesion (6.1) and at the role non-governmental actors play (6.2).

6.1 Governmental actors

Throughout Europe governments, and more in particular the legislative and executive branches, are re-examining and modifying their roles in response to rapid changes in the region's economic landscape. The general trend towards privatisation and deregulation has been accompanied by devolution in the authority and responsibility for integration matters to regional and local governments and to a wider group of non-governmental actors. At the same time, international and supra-national co-operation has become of greater importance. This and a pragmatic assessment of the limits of government in social and economic life has precipitated an increasing openness on the part of governments to enlist the support and advice of the non-governmental actors in developing strategies aimed at combating socio-economic exclusion of immigrants and minorities.

Notwithstanding the fact that many governments are redefining their role and the degree of their involvement, they continue to have three identifiable roles, namely as legislator, facilitator and as setting examples.

Government as legislator

National parliaments are using their legislative powers to propose and enact legislation in the fields of residence rights, the promotion of equal treatment, nationality and anti-discrimination. They also translate international human rights obligations into national law and set enforceable standards. Decentralisation provides a framework for the partial transfer of legislative powers to regional and local authorities. National and regional parliaments and city councils monitor the implementation of policies concerning immigrants and minorities.

At present there is much debate on the question of the degree of legislative intervention on matters related to equal treatment of immigrants and minorities, anti-discrimination and positive action. It is important to make a distinction between positive discrimination and positive action. Positive action is applied when policies are adopted, in principle for a period limited in time, which target specific groups, regions or cities in which certain groups tends to concentrate, with a view to enable these groups to participate in or profit equally from governmental programmes and services. Such action is in particular necessary when certain groups experience multiple and cumulative disadvantages which are unique to these communities. Positive action is, nationally and internationally, an accepted principle. Positive discrimination defined as giving preferential treatment to certain ethnic groups, by law and for an unlimited period, clashes with European principles of equality.

To the extent that European states regulate the practices of employment and service provision, it is primarily in the area of prohibiting discrimination. Discrimination is made an offence under criminal law and in fewer instances under civil law or a combination of the two. The monitoring of the effective implementation of such legislation is crucial, as is the active role of the judiciary to punish non-observance of the law.

The persistence of direct and indirect discriminatory practices towards immigrants and minorities and the commitment to become more democratic and inclusive societies, have lead to calls to adopt more stringent legislative measures designed to regulate the practices of employers and institutions that provide services (such as housing and education). The resistance against such measures is great. Employers and service providers maintain that such measures complicate matters instead of bringing solutions. Trade unions maintain that such measures could divide workers and create tensions on the shop floor. Many immigrants and minorities argue that companies and government offices should not employ or provide services to immigrants and minorities to fill quotas, but rather, they should "employ the right people".

It is important to distinguish between legislation that punishes discriminatory acts and behaviour (anti-discrimination legislation) and legislation that seeks to "level the playing field" by encouraging companies to employ qualified immigrants and minorities (target setting). Those who are opposed to these forms of government regulation usually agreed that it is useful to have legislation that punishes discrimination. Legislation which goes further than that may not be the solution, there are nevertheless many examples where the threat of such legislation has prompted companies to act on a voluntary basis by adopting recruitment and promotion policies which reflect more the population in the locales in which they operate. Voluntary target setting is increasingly being viewed as a reasonable, business-like approach to finding qualified immigrants or minorities for vacant positions. The commitment fostered through voluntary development and/or participation in various initiatives could be much more effective and more likely to endure than arrangements imposed by legislation.

Government as facilitator

Executive branches of government should facilitate co-operation between the various governmental departments and agencies, the various levels of government and relevant actors. Matters related to immigrants and minorities usually fall within the mandate of various ministries: interior, justice, public order, health, social affairs, employment, housing, etc. Co-operation between these ministries avoids inconsistencies in policies and uncertainties among the immigrant and minority population. A clear division of labour between the national, regional and local levels of government enhances the effectiveness of governmental action.

There are many examples of national governments taking a leading role in the co-ordination of co-operation between regional and local authorities. Governments should facilitate co-operation and consultation between governments and non-governmental actors and between these actors. Governments can initiate and finance policy oriented research.

Governments can promote diversity and cohesion by other measures such as making resources available to municipal authorities, supporting and subsidising the activities of non-governmental actors, and promoting dialogues and partnerships between key social actors.

Government as example

Governments, both the legislative and executive branches, can act as an example by making public statements on the contribution immigrants and minorities make to society and by condemning discrimination.

While most government positions in Europe are reserved for country nationals (including naturalised citizens), many naturalised and second- and third-generation immigrants and minorities suffer from discriminatory treatment or face other barriers to employment in the government sector, just as they do in the private sector. National and local governments are employers and can increase access to governmental positions for immigrants and minorities. As with any place of employment, government offices also need to institute their own internal review of recruitment procedures to remove any direct or indirect barriers to immigrant or minority participation. This is not only important in demonstrating leadership and reinforcing principles of equal opportunity, but it will also enable these offices to draw upon the skills and talents of a broad range of qualified individuals. This can be achieved by attempting to reflect the multicultural character of the community in government offices; redefining criteria in assessing suitability for the job; revising communication strategies for publicising positions; participating in mentoring schemes with minority staff and/or community members; and setting voluntary targets for recruitment and promotion.

National and local governments can ensure the professional development of immigrant and minority staff. As in many corporate offices, immigrant and minority staff in government and parliamentary offices tends to be concentrated in lower-grade and lower-skilled positions. Government offices are well positioned; however, to develop the professional capacities of their immigrants and minority employees through many similar practices employed by private companies. In addition to mentoring schemes that pair senior and junior minority staff, government offices can benefit from training sessions, which enable immigrants and minority staff to discuss with one another their professional development and their own skill and training needs.

National and local government can prepare the government office for a diverse employee base. These offices will also gain from modification of internal practices to better accommodate a diverse employee base. This will ensure that these offices do not favour only those immigrants and minorities who are able or willing to acclimate to the existing workplace "culture". Organisational change that is adapted for greater social and cultural diversity can include: diversity management training for managers; intercultural training for non-managerial staff; the establishment of mechanisms for dealing with racial and ethnic harassment; and demonstrating openness for cultural and ethnic difference.

As with the private sector, national and local governments can play a significant role in enhancing the economic foundation of disadvantaged communities by identifying and including immigrant and minority-owned businesses in tender lists for supplies and services. Some governmental offices are considering to engage in further discussions about possible experimentation with variations of the American "contract compliance" programme, such as setting voluntary targets for contracts with immigrants and minority entrepreneurs and/or sub-contracting with those companies who themselves contract with immigrant and minority enterprises.

The examples of government acting as legislator, facilitator and example show that governments play a vital role in promoting diversity and cohesion. This is not to say that governments are always assuming their full responsibilities in this regard. They may even contribute to problems surrounding the inclusion of immigrants and minorities, for example, by failing to take the appropriate legal measures, by not providing the necessary resources for other measures, or by becoming an instrument of extremist ideas and political movements.

6.2   Non-governmental actors

The integration of immigrants and minorities into society cannot be achieved without the active involvement of non-governmental actors. In some parts of Europe these actors have played this important role already for many years. Where in other parts of Europe the development of civil society is actively promoted, non-governmental organisations will need to be assisted to assume a similar role. There is still need for further discussion and negotiation among the various actors to define their respective roles. Both governmental and non-governmental actors are aware that their co-operation is crucial in a civil society.

There exist a broad range of non-governmental actors. Among them are organisations with a wide brief that includes immigrant and minority issues. Others are highly specialised institutes or single-issue organisations. Their status may vary and ranges from well-established institutes to grass-roots organisations. Some organisations work exclusively at the local level, others at the national and international levels. In many European countries, a well-developed voluntary sector exists which plays a crucial role in the integration of immigrants and minorities. Volunteers are also heavily involved in the work of such professional organisations as political parties, trade unions and religious organisations.

Immigrants and minorities have the mutual not exclusive option to create their own organisations or to join the mainstream or majority organisations to defend their rights and to promote their integration into society. The activities of immigrant and minority organisations can compliment the participation in mainstream or majority organisations. Sometimes immigrant and minority organisations have more limited aims and are more focussed and flexible in achieving them, whereas the mainstream or majority organisations combine the aims of a greater variety of people and represent more power to achieve them.

There are organisations based on the national origin of immigrants or on the ethnic origin of minorities, as well as organisations with a broader national and ethnic membership base. Their aims are either social, cultural or both. Immigrants and minorities may create their own political parties, trade unions or professional organisations, and churches and religious organisations. Immigrant and minority organisations may acquire the status of an official counterpart of governments.

By promoting diversity and cohesion in society, non-governmental actors must apply to themselves the principles underlying cultural pluralism, namely: equality, tolerance and anti-discrimination. Not every organisation, however, is willing to make the challenge of a diverse society a challenge for itself. Non-governmental actors can also be exclusive and reinforce, in subtle ways, prejudices towards others.

There are also strong forces in society that reject diversity. Social movements, political parties, churches and other organisations – including those of immigrants and minorities – may reject cultural pluralism and promote intolerance towards people with a different ethnic or national origin or skin colour.

Political parties

In democratic societies political parties have a variety of tasks and responsibilities. They defend and act according to the principles of democratic societies. They provide a platform for debates on issues where consensus can be reached or where differences of opinion reflect the conflicting interests of groups in society. They voice the concerns of their constituency and demonstrate leadership by taking position and project a vision on society's future. Another important function of political parties is the recruitment people for the actively participation in the political process. In many countries the inclusion of immigrants and minorities has traditionally been an important instrument to involve these persons with democratic principles and to integrate them into this mainstream institution. This facilitated also the inclusion of matters of concern to immigrants and minorities in the life of political parties. Immigrants and minorities have also founded their own political parties, which often were effective instruments to defend their interests.

In the name of democratic principles political parties should reject openly any form of racial and ethnic discrimination and condemn intolerance and incitement to racial hatred. They could also refuse to distribute or endorse views and positions that stir up or invite prejudices, hostility or division between people of different ethnic or national origin, religion and belief and skin colour. Parties can fight against all forms of racial discrimination within their own ranks.

During electoral campaigns issues related to immigrants and minorities should be dealt with in a responsible way. Without ignoring or belittling the problems related to the integration of immigrants and minorities, political parties could stress the positive sides of diversity and cultural pluralism. Awareness of those issues and the sensitivities surrounding them could be parts of the screening process of candidates running for public office. Furthermore, parties can publicly state that they will not co-operate with extremist parties or form governments with them.

It is also of great importance that persons belonging to the groups of immigrants and minorities are represented at all level in the parties. Political parties could adopt an active policy to recruit them as members, involve them in the life of the party and select them as candidates for public and other offices.

The private sector

A combination of often-overlapping social and commercial factors augments a growing business stake in the inclusion of Europe's immigrants and minorities. As immigrant and minority populations continue to concentrate in urban centres throughout Europe, their participation in the labour force and enterprise development has become part of a larger business necessity in servicing a cultural and racial divers community and client base.

For many companies, a key motivation for engaging in initiatives in the area of societal integration stems from a variety of principles often referred to as "corporate responsibility" or "corporate citizenship". As members of society, business can and ought to contribute to the development and maintenance of healthy communities. Many firms are discovering that they may obtain a number of commercial benefits from developing reputations as socially responsible companies. In an age of increasing consumer scrutiny, cause-related marketing aimed at combating long-term unemployment or environmental rehabilitation, for example, can foster a positive public image for the company among public and private consumers, community groups, current and future employees. It is increasingly understood that consumers are no longer exclusively buying products and services, but the actual companies – or corporate images – behind them. Several initiatives in the area of diversity are thus part of an overall, carefully crafted corporate strategy to become the "supplier..." "producer..." "investment..." and/or "employer of choice".

Often and increasingly, the motivation for corporate action in the area of socio-economic inclusion of immigrants and minorities stems from some combination of "enlightened self-interest", socially responsible activities which result in tangible business gains, or "win-win strategies" for the company and larger society.

The changing profile of local labour markets (culturally and ethnically diverse) demands the recognition and development of the skills and potential of personnel who, regardless of background, feel valued and motivated to work efficiently and productively can add flexibility and innovation to the company workforce. As immigrant and minority communities in Europe continue to grow, they constitute new and underdeveloped markets for goods and services. In addition, they may present marketing opportunities for the development of a broad range of new products and services.

An idea gaining increasing support in business circles suggests that work teams comprised of persons from diverse backgrounds can bring added value to business activities through increased creativity and problem-solving capacity. There is also growing recognition that many second- and third-generation immigrants and minorities offer a degree of flexibility and innovation that may stem from living in more than one culture. With little competitive advantage in the area of price and quality, innovation may be the edge European companies can strive for.

Country-of-origin links, diverse language skills, knowledge of and direct access to international markets, are only a few of the competitive advantages offered by members of immigrant and minority communities to those companies who are willing to make use of such "insider knowledge".

In addition to direct benefits to the company achieved through socially driven initiatives, there are a number of larger societal "by-products" of such schemes. Efforts to augment the employment opportunities of marginalised immigrant and minority communities provide an important pathway to their integration, helping to strengthen social cohesion, and thus producing stable societies in which to conduct business.

Trade unions

Traditionally trade unions have been involved in many activities aimed at the protection of the rights and dignity of migrant workers and their families. They work actively to promote the equal treatment of migrant workers with national workers in matters of recruitment, working and living conditions and education, as well as on concrete initiatives designed to combat racial harassment and discrimination in the work place.

While trade unions may have lost their previously strong position in some sectors, they are nevertheless well positioned to develop and support measures aimed at combating racial harassment and discrimination, as well as those, which promote equal treatment in personnel policies. Because the work floor is often the first place that immigrants and minorities encounter a new society, trade unions have been key in (co-) organising language and other training courses, as well as intercultural training for their majority members. In order to be more effective in these areas, many trade unions have sought to broaden their membership base to include immigrant and minority workers. In this way, trade unions try – with varying degrees of success – to challenge the perception that they exclusively defend the interests of majority workers.

Trade unions have played and are playing an equally important role in shaping or influencing policies at the European, national and local levels, and often as partners in official structures which also include employers' organisations. Where such formalised co-operation between trade unions and employers organisations (the so-called social partners) exists, it has helped to produce important measures. They include the adoption of joint declarations and/or codes of conducts on the prevention of racial and ethnic discrimination and voluntary agreements on the establishment of targets for immigrant and minority recruitment. In some sectors, concrete activities are being jointly undertaken by the social partners aimed at promoting intercultural understanding and harmonious relations among a diverse workforce.

Churches and other faith communities

Christian churches and other faith communities play their own role in the integration of immigrants and minorities. For many Christians among the immigrant population, churches offer a first entry into the receiving society. Mosques and temples play the same role for many Moslems and Hindus. Churches and other faith communities often speak with authority on the necessity to protect the rights of immigrants and minorities and in favour of adequate measures to accommodate their needs. They condemn violations of human rights and racist acts and attitudes.

Religious organisations are in numerous ways involved in practical work supporting immigrants and minorities. They offer professional social assistance often accompanied by other forms of aid by volunteers. They intervene in conflict situations between immigrant or minority groups and the majority population, and voice the concerns of oppressed minorities. As part of their work to assist socially excluded people, they appeal to policy-makers and politicians without making politically partisan statements. They offer financial support to all kinds of activities organised by immigrant and minority associations or other NGOs. In some countries, churches offer protection to irregular migrants (so-called church asylum).

Non-governmental organisations

Non-governmental organisations (NGOs) play an important role in promoting the integration of immigrants and minorities. A distinction can be made between varying types of NGOs. Firstly, there are quasi-governmental bodies that principally focus on the statutory context or serve as an official platform of dialogue between governments and minority organisations. Secondly, in most European countries there are immigrant and minority assistance/aid organisations. These voluntary organisations are involved in the reception of newcomers and assist immigrants and minorities in all sorts of ways with the integration into society. They support immigrants and minorities when they claim their rights before courts and assist them in taking legal action against discrimination. More established organisations work closely together with governments and often are contracted by governments to carry out specific programmes. Thirdly, there are advocacy organisations. These organisations monitor national policies and the implementation international human rights standards. They can embarrass governments by publishing their findings in national and international forums, often leading to policy changes and compliance with international standards. Advocacy organisations not only want to be involved in the implementation of governmental policies, but also in the process of policy formation. They raise public awareness of the often-precarious situation of immigrants and minorities and present and press for concrete proposals to improve that situation. Fifthly, there are single-issue organisations that conduct public and policy campaigns on specific concerns with regard to the position of immigrants and minorities.

Governments recognise the important role NGOs are playing and often urge these organisations to take on more responsibilities. This is not to say that governments and NGOs do not have different views and opinions that, at times, lead to the interruption of the dialogue and co-operation between them.

In some parts of Europe, NGOs often do not have the capacity to assume more tasks. Sometimes they are only active in the capitals, whereas they are needed in smaller towns; sometimes they limit themselves to political issues related to migration and are to a much lesser extent involved in practical work. In Eastern Europe, NGOs are asking governments to assume greater financial responsibility for their work so that the financial dependence on foreign donors could gradually be reduced. They also stress the need to provide a legislative framework that defines the role and status of NGOs. In some Eastern European countries, international NGOs have stepped in where no national NGOs existed.

Artists and intellectuals

Artist and intellectuals often voice independent and dissenting views and take position in defence of civil liberties and cultural diversity. They can denounce violations of human rights and racism and mobilise public support for immigrants and minorities. In addition, artists and intellectuals can broaden perspectives, reflect on the fundamental changes in modern society and develop a vision for the future. Through their work, scientists and scientific institutions can contribute to a well-informed policy debate. The community of artists, intellectuals and scientists count many who have a migrant background or belong to a minority.

Sports

The role of sport in promoting social integration, in particular of young people, is widely recognised. Sport has become more than just a leisure pursuit. It is a recognised social phenomenon. Sports offer a common language and a platform for social democracy. It creates conditions for political democracy and is instrumental to the development of democratic citizenship. Sport enhances the understanding and appreciation of cultural differences and it contributes to the fight against prejudices. Finally, sport plays its part to limit social exclusion of immigrant and minority groups[1].

---

1. Social cohesion and sport. Examples of good practice from member countries of the Committee for the Development of Sport (Council of Europe, 1999).

Chapter VII: Promoting cohesion by valuing diversity

This chapter will give examples of governmental and non-governmental policies and practices on socio-economic inclusion (7.1 – 7.4), cultural diversity (7.5 – 7.9) and political participation (7.10).

7.1 Business initiatives

A significant number of companies are modifying their internal practices to access the opportunities presented by immigrant and minority communities. These changes include the identification of qualified immigrant and minority personnel in recruitment; the professional development of existing migrant and minority staff to ensure their internal mobility (to higher-skilled or higher-status positions); and the adaptation of the organisational culture for inclusion of employees from different backgrounds. These programmes may also give special attention to immigrant and minority women.

Firms are discovering the benefits of recruiting from immigrant and minority communities, whether this stems from removing barriers to accessing highly skilled persons, or more generally, from operating in urban environments inhabited by large populations of economically active persons and consumers. Several firms are deriving direct and indirect benefits by undertaking a commitment to reflect their local communities' ethnic/cultural make-up in the companies' work force. Many companies begin to discover that through modification – and not lowering – of employment criteria, they are better able to draw upon the skills and talents of a diverse employee base in meeting their business needs. For example, while most firms still insist on a minimum of language-proficiency, the benefits of employing bilingual or multilingual speaking employees are obvious for firms seeking to develop new markets.

Even those companies that are predisposed towards recruiting immigrants or minorities often complain that such individuals rarely apply for advertised positions. This suggests that traditional ways of publicising vacancies – both internally and externally – are less effective in attracting suitable applicants of immigrant or minority background. Merely stating that one is "an equal opportunity employer" does not necessarily remove the detectable or hidden impediments to identifying qualified immigrant or minority applicants. A number of employers have devised particular strategies for increasing applications of these groups. This ranges from more subtle approaches, such as featuring minority faces in company publications and commercials to more active methods such as establishing data base which match unemployed members of immigrant or minority communities with firms looking to fill vacancies.

A common and successful method employed by businesses to increase labour market access and promotion opportunities for excluded groups is through mentoring schemes that match immigrant and minority "mentees" with "mentor" staff persons within the firm. The mentoring schemes typically run from three to twelve months, consisting of several weeks of core curriculum, and several more weeks of practical application under the tutelage of a company staff person.

One of the most basic means of facilitating access to employment for excluded groups is through setting targets for their recruitment. Many companies do this informally by instructing personnel managers to ensure that the work force composition closely approximates that of the local communities. Other companies have taken a more active stance to ensure that targets are reached. Target setting needs to be accompanied by a clear understanding that recruitment should only be based on merit. Recruiters can then give priority to the identification of suitable immigrants or minorities who are assessed on the basis of their competence and aptitudes, rather than engaging in (counter-productive) attempts to meet the numerical targets by recruiting people who do not have appropriate competences. Such measures have also helped some firms rehabilitate a tarnished public image derived from past charges of discrimination.

Even where immigrants and minorities are present in the work force of large companies, they tend to be concentrated in lower-grade positions. This may occur because immigrant and minority staff has particular training needs, or as a consequence of the working procedures of the firm, or from direct or indirect discriminatory practices. Thus, even in instances where minority staff has the skills and potential for higher-grade positions, barriers to progress may still arise within the organisation. This applies in particular to immigrant or minority women and young people. Each company must therefore ascertain the reasons for the under-representation of immigrants or minorities in senior positions in order to identify the most appropriate strategy for staff development in that company.

A significant factor in determining companies' gains from diversity has to do with how this diversity is managed within the firm, and more generally, how the company adapts to its diverse workforce. Firms which strive to treat all staff equally, such that all colour and ethnic differences are ignored – 'the colour-blind approach' – do not always recognise the extent to which established corporate practices indirectly discriminate against certain employees. In companies where little is done to modify practices to better accommodate a diverse employee base, only those minorities who are able or willing to acclimate to the existing corporate "culture" are likely to persist and progress.

The expectation that new minority staff fits into the existing organisation with little organisational change to accommodate greater social and cultural diversity, can result in loss to the organisation of the talent and skills of the full range of potential employees. It also means a loss to the organisation of creative ideas and problem solving from the varied perspectives of people of different backgrounds; finally, it is a loss to minority personnel, who consequently find themselves concentrated in low-grade or low-status jobs with mobility blocked by invisible barriers.

Adapting the firm in such a way as to maximise the potential contributions of the entire workforce usually involves the support of the chief executive and senior managers. It requires the re-evaluation of personnel policies and procedures to identify actual or potential sources of adverse impact against employees of different backgrounds. In addition it requires the training of personnel and the introduction of procedures designed to create an atmosphere of openness and to encourage feedback from the entire workforce.

Another key component of adapting the firm for a diverse workforce is the introduction of policies and mechanisms to deal with racial and ethnic harassment in the work place. Explicit policies setting out the standards of behaviour expected in the workplace and identifying those which undermine the dignity of staff (such as racist jokes or comments) make it clear to employees that the company values all of its workers. Such policies are accompanied by informal and formal complaint procedures in which those employees who feel they have been harassed may raise their concerns without fear of penalty or other negative consequences. Some companies have chosen to demonstrate their commitment to the prevention of racial discrimination through collective agreements and the establishment of voluntary codes of conduct or good practice. A good example of the latter is the Joint Declaration on the Prevention of Racial Discrimination and Xenophobia and Promotion of Equal Treatment at the Workplace. The European Social Partners, being the European employers' organisations and European trade union organisation have adopted this Declaration. Often lessons acquired in the area of gender discrimination are applied to fight racial and ethnic discrimination.

Because they operate in social environments, companies have a keen interest in ensuring that such communities are stable and prosperous. Businesses throughout Europe are undertaking a number of "social investment" initiatives or are otherwise acting to support immigrant and minority communities for a variety of possible objectives. First, to improve the corporate image in minority communities in order to attract new employees, customers and clients. Second, to support the development and inclusion of minority communities as part of the wider social responsibility of business. Third, to prepare the next generation of workers. Fourth, to develop business partnerships with minority-owned businesses to address their exclusion from the wider economic development of the region.

Business action in local communities can take a variety of forms, including programmes to educate immigrant and minority youth, the creation of corporate foundations to fund social projects, and support for and/or liasing with other organisations which seek to further business involvement in social projects. Business engagement can encompass a variety of actions, such as urban regeneration strategies, ensuring the provision of public services in depressed neighbourhoods, housing projects and beautification schemes. This engagement can range from fiscal support for community projects to actual corporate donations of time, in the form of mentorship or other guidance programmes. Finally, because of their prominence and visibility in local communities, companies are well positioned to promote positive images of migrants and minorities, and to condemn racist and xenophobic acts and attitudes.

7.2 Immigrant and minority business

Several factors point to the growing significance of immigrant and minority enterprise in Europe. It is an alternative to wage labour, unemployment and public assistance, it is a benefit to local and national economies, and it is a pathway to socio-economic integration.

Contemporary economic developments have disproportionately affected Europe's immigrant and minority residents, augmenting the importance of self-employment as a viable means of economic activity for persons with diminishing opportunities in the current labour market. With Europe's industrial base in decline, immigrant and minority business is providing a channel through which such individuals may participate in the economic life of their communities and divert the costly consequences of marginalisation.

In some European countries, immigrants and minorities constitute higher rates of self-employment than national populations. In addition, some individuals from migrant communities are often cited for their "entrepreneurial" traits, most notably their tendency to take risks and to be self-reliant. Among these entrepreneurs are many women. There are several other ways in which immigrant and minority enterprises are contributing to local and national economies throughout Europe. First, immigrant and minority businesses generate thousands of jobs every year. In addition to alleviating some of the pressure on local labour markets, they also account for the annual creation of hundreds of new types of businesses. Second, in contrast to the public perception that immigrants and minorities depress neighbourhood conditions, studies indicate that immigrant and minority businesses often turn disadvantaged areas into commercial zones and can become a source of new economic life for urban communities. By renting and renovating space and supplying goods and services to Europe's expanding immigrant and minority population, these businesses can provide new forms of wealth for minority urban-dwelling populations. Third, in addition to expanding into under-served markets, immigrant and minority owned businesses generate economic growth through the purchasing of equipment and products, the provision of additional employment opportunities, and the utilisation of links with countries of origin to stimulate import-export trade. Some studies have also credited these businesses for stimulating growth in the diminishing small business sector.

Whether a consequence of exclusion from mainstream economies or a by-product of the human capital these populations often exhibit, entrepreneurship is attributing to the commercial success of many of Europe's resident immigrants and minorities. Moreover, economic participation – which enables such individuals to assume a greater degree of financial independence and self-sufficiency – is an important element in their integration into larger society. In particular, entrepreneurship may help to address the aspirations of second- and third-generation immigrants and other minority youth who are not willing to accept exclusion from mainstream institutions. Local communities gain both economically and socially from the resourceful participation of resident populations.

National and local governments can support this type of entrepreneurship by providing for training tailored to the specific needs of women and young entrepreneurs, assisting entrepreneurs to comply with national labour laws, removing unnecessary legal obstacles for entrepreneurs and offering them business contracts. Governments could also establish an award for successful entrepreneurs.

7.3 Area based policies

International migration has its most tangible and visible effect at the local level, where the challenges of diversity and cohesion are most readily felt. The urban policy agenda will show many items related to diversity and cohesion. In many countries, local and regional governments – including those operating in rural areas – have put integration policies in place. National governments have given local and regional authorities more responsibilities, but not always the necessary means to carry out effective integration policies. Even when many policy are within the domain of local and regional governments, national governments intervention is still needed to ensure that immigrants and minorities benefit from the often scarce public goods in cases that socio-economically disadvantaged persons compete for these goods.

With the onset of recession and increasing globalisation, cities in Europe began to experience decline, spawning a series of governmental recovery programmes to replace declining industries with more competitive ones and to improve local infrastructure. Immigrants and minorities, often concentrated in the poorer neighbourhoods, were in most cases the greatest victims of these broad-based economic recovery and structural adjustment policies.

While poorer areas had always existed in European cities, these pockets of deprivation worsened in the 1980s, and were characterised by worsening levels of long-term unemployment or under-employment, concentrated poverty, low educational attainment, poor housing, and high social welfare dependency among their immigrant and minority residents. Concepts such as the "divided city" and "spatial segregation" began to enter the lexicon of urban policy planners and policy-makers.

National and local governments have searched for solutions to this phenomenon through a variety of policy responses designed to renovate neighbourhoods, develop human resources, attract investment and reduce unemployment. They have sought to ameliorate the conditions of urban race/ethnicity-impacted poverty through social assistance schemes designed to meet individual needs. As unemployment numbers have continued to rise, the growing public costs of this approach and their failure to break cycles of dependence and deprivation has pointed to the need for new policy directions. Sectional-based policies have sought to address the particular elements of depressed urban areas through different governmental departments and emphases, such as improved housing, job training and work experience, education, enterprise development, etc. Though not without effect, such policy responses were too limited or ad hoc and failed to address the multidimensional and interdependent causes of concentrated deprivation and exclusion.

Governments have also sought to involve the private sector in tackling the problems of urban deprivation through various incentive schemes. On the human resource development side, this has included subsidised work-experience for long-term unemployed and other mentoring schemes. On the economic development-side, some European governments have used tax incentives and other financial inducements to attract new investment into areas of industrial decline. While in some cases successful in attracting investment in certain run-down areas, depressed urban neighbourhoods have generally not benefited from such zone schemes.

In several European countries there is currently is a move towards area-based strategies. Several European national governments began to devolve authority and resources to local governments to address the problems of depressed urban areas. While central governments continued to outline the framework for action, initiatives of national governments offered municipal authorities flexibility in co-ordinating local solutions to address the conditions of neighbourhood-based socio-economic exclusion. The most significant and common aspect of these policy approaches was their targeting of specific geographical areas (usually determined on the basis of a series of social and economic indicators) and their partnering of central and local authorities.

The challenge for central and city governments remains the identification of an appropriate mix of targeted social and economic actions to bring these areas up to a level less distinct from their surrounding areas, and to restore economic and other opportunities for their diverse residents. The multidimensional causes of deprived urban areas have also spawned awareness that urban policy cannot be dealt with as merely an aggregation of ad hoc policy domains, but must be integrated with other policy areas such as employment, environment, social welfare and education. This need to bridge economic and social development goals is requiring a more co-ordinated and integrated approach between the different branches and levels of government. Rather than uncoordinated and isolated policy responses, the interdependency of these areas is calling for greater linkage of programmes that address physical infrastructure, human resource development and the integration of excluded groups.

Although "partnership" has in some cases been an over-used or abused concept in the discussions of urban policy, there is growing awareness of the need to involve additional stakeholders in the formulation of local responses to neighbourhood decline. While the capacity of many non-governmental actors to adequately address the multiple challenges in depressed urban areas has been limited, they are proving to be an invaluable partner in informing and delivering initiatives in critical areas. Such "bottom up" approaches call for the involvement of a broad base of community actors, non-profit and non-governmental organisations, local authorities, religious organisations and others to work towards local solutions based on common visions of what they want their communities to be. A number of European and central funding schemes have made cross-sectorial "partnership" an essential criterion in awarding grants to specific urban regeneration bids.

One of the more successful efforts to enlist private sector involvement in depressed urban areas has been through the redevelopment of specific "brown field" lands, often located in disadvantaged central city areas. In some cities, the promotion of minority business development is emerging as an area of increasing importance for both human resource and urban economic development. Although many minority-owned businesses are catering to under-served city markets (with substantial buying power), strategic thinking in some cities is linking the expansion of immigrant and minority business to larger metropolitan and regional economic development.

Urban renewal scenarios arise out of policy choices[1]. They should be developed through widespread consultation with communities, key actors in the public and private sectors and opinion leaders in the media and community affairs. Each scenario should describe a focus or sector of interest, and each has its related implementation projects. Together they form a matrix within which combinations of choices can be made and new ideas and options can

1. This and the following paragraph are based on *Area-based projects in districts of high immigrant concentration* (Council of Europe, 1996).

be further identified. They are formulated to address the needs of the local population as a whole, and to promote integration and equal opportunities where immigrants and minorities are concerned. Such policies and projects should foster the active participation by immigrants and minorities in defining their needs and in the restructuring of local neighbourhoods. This would enhance the policies' effectiveness and strengthens the ability of people to manage change and conflict accompanying urban renewal.

Urban development should contribute towards attaining equal opportunity and tackle specified inequalities. It requires special arrangements to meet cultural, religious or communication needs. In addition, urban policies have to pay special attention to the problems of the second and third generation families and their children. Urban projects can help raise the profile of immigrant and minority women and give expression to their views and demands. These individuals play a role in designing, developing and organising urban projects and be involved in the management of the projects. An award to cities or mayors with the most active and effective integration policies could be developed.

Although in many cases the majority of immigrants and minorities are settled in urban areas, there are also many living in rural areas. Specific policies are needed to address this situation, while many elements of urban policies can also be adapted and applied to rural areas.

7.4 Governmental initiatives

In most European countries national and local governments are involved in initiatives to incorporate immigrants and minorities into the labour market and/or to include these groups in economic development. Examples of these policies and practices have been given in the previous sections of this chapter.

As legislator governments provide for a legal environment in which economic activities can be undertaken. Governments are also setting labour standards and promote equal treatment by the adoption of anti-discrimination legislation. Governments can also remove legal and bureaucratic barriers for the full participation of immigrants and minorities in economic life, either as employee, self-employed or entrepreneur. As facilitator governments can provide for education and financial support for immigrant and minority entrepreneurs. Special attention needs to be given to persons who are facing cumulative disadvantages (young people with an immigrant or minority background) or double discrimination (such as immigrant and minority women). Governments can also conclude private and public partnerships aimed at the regeneration of neighbourhoods and job creation. Labour offices, often (semi-) official institutions can give special attention to groups that have difficulties in entering the labour market, either because of the lack of the required skills or because of discrimination. As an employer governments can adopt similar employment strategies, as are employed in the private sector. Governments have also purchasing power and can include immigrants and minority businesses as their supplier.

7.5 Intercultural dialogue and education

The importance of cultural co-operation and intercultural dialogue is recognised by many European governments. The 6th Conference of European Ministers for Cultural Affairs stated that the richness of European culture stems from the diversity and vitality of its national, regional and local cultures and from its openness to influences from other parts of the world[1]. According to the ministers, people have the duty to preserve and promote what makes them different and at the same time be aware of a common European culture and heritage. The preservation of diversity is inconceivable in a climate of withdrawal and isolation. Dialogue between cultures is vital for the further development of Europe. The Ministers Conference decided to promote better access for the whole population to European culture and heritage, to foster the identity and self-expression of individuals and communities, and to encourage co-operation and dialogue between cultures.

The Ministers Conference recognised that diversity poses a challenge to cohesion and presents an opportunity to fulfil Europe's ideals. Cultural co-operation can achieve a harmonious balance between minority identities and culture and can provide access to Europe's common cultural heritage. The Final Declaration of the Summit of Heads of State and Government states that cultural co-operation is essential for creating a cohesive yet diverse Europe[2].

The Ministers Conference considered the diversity of European cultures. In addition, they recognised that migrants bring their own cultural heritage and add to Europe's diversity. In another Council of Europe context, cultures of national minorities are expressly valued. The Framework Convention for the Protection of National Minorities obliges contracting parties to promote the conditions necessary for persons belonging to national minorities to maintain and develop their culture, and to preserve the essential elements of their identity, namely their religion, language, traditions and cultural heritage. The contracting parties shall refrain from policies or practices aimed at forced assimilation of persons belonging to national minorities. The Preamble of the Charter for Regional and Minority Languages stresses the value of cultural diversity, interculturalism and multilingualism.

Whereas the cultural identity of and the diversity among majority or dominant groups are recognised and cultural pluralism is valued, immigrants and minorities are often expected to assimilate to a dominant culture or give up essential components of their own culture. Governments should include

---

1. Sixth Conference of European Ministers for Cultural Affairs (Palermo, 1990).
2. Final Declaration of the Summit of Heads of State and Government (Vienna, 1993).

immigrant and minority cultures in their general policies to preserve cultural pluralism and to promote cultural co-operation (mainstreaming). There are various ways by which governments can achieve this[1].

The lawful recognition of diversity and minority groups lays the foundation for cultural co-operation and dialogue. Constitutions of many European states contain the recognition of minority groups (which are often mentioned by name). Even more Constitutions establish principles of equality and anti-discrimination, which also apply to the cultural field. Secondary legislation spells out cultural rights in much more detail. In some countries minorities are cultural autonomous and given the power, institutions and other resources to decide on cultural and educational matters without interference by the national government. The recognition of minority languages, also in official contacts with the various governmental levels and the judiciary, is another way of preserving cultural pluralism.

Cultural identity should be understood as dynamic and evolving. Identity cannot be reduced to a set of unchanging cultural determinants to which persons and groups are subject by virtue of their national or ethnic origin or birth. Identity can neither be protected by isolation from the surrounding society or with no regard for the relationship with universal values of human rights. Governmental policies can support the development of immigrant and minority cultures by, among other means, subsidising their cultural activities, opening up mainstream cultural facilities and inviting these groups to participate in the formation of cultural policies.

The fact that individuals have multiple identities and affiliations links them with a variety of groups and institutions. This greatly contributes to social cohesion. Governments can create conditions that prevent specific groups from becoming isolated and individuals' options to participate in society from being reduced, and ensure that their contributions are valued by opening up mainstream institutions for immigrants and minorities.

A new and fresh approach to history must represent the perspectives of the various groups in society and different views should be compared and brought together[2]. This would enhance mutual understanding and respect and dispel stereotypes and prejudices, between majority and minority and among minorities. The promotion of human rights is also considered to be central to cultural and educational policies. Governments can stimulate the development of programmes that educate caring and responsible citizens to respect human rights and dignity, to be open to cultures and appreciative of

---

1. The following four paragraphs are based on: the Council of Europe's project on Democracy, human rights, minorities: educational and cultural aspects (1997) and *Human Rights and minorities in the new European democracies: educational and cultural aspects* (Strasbourg, 1994).
2. See also *Lessons in history, the Council of Europe and the teaching of history*, Council of Europe, 1999.

differences, and to seek non-violent solutions for conflicts. Civic education cannot be limited to curricula or textbooks but should also be based on practical experiences and possibilities for active participation and empowerment of citizens. In such an active dialogue, shared values are reconfirmed and some are given new meanings. This process will increase the acceptance of these values by a diverse population.

Language and education

The Charter on Regional and Minority Languages' overriding purpose is cultural and designed to protect and promote regional or minority languages that have been spoken over a long period in Europe. Their eventual extinction was considered to be a threat to Europe's cultural heritage.

Member states are required to take into account the reality of cultural and linguistic plurality. However, this may not be interpreted as a challenge to national sovereignty and territorial integrity. Enhancing the possibilities of using regional or minority languages can encourage the groups who speak them to participate in society. This should not be detrimental to the official languages and the need to learn them. The formation of linguistic ghettos must be avoided as being contrary to the principles of interculturalism and multilingualism[1].

Governments should make available (a substantial part of) pre-school education, primary and secondary education, technical and vocational education, and university and higher education in regional or minority languages. Governments should provide this at least for those pupils whose families so request and, in the cases of higher education, for students when they so request. Their numbers must be considered as sufficient, meaning that it cannot be required from the public authorities to provide such education when there are not enough pupils/students to form a class. However, it is suggested that this criteria is applied in a flexible way and that a lower number may be considered as sufficient. When public authorities have no direct competence in pre-school education, they can encouraged the responsible organisations to teach regional or minority languages. Universities and higher and adult education institutions could provide facilities for the study of regional or minority languages. Governments can provide the basic and further training of the teachers and make the necessary means available in terms of finance, staff and teaching aids. Finally, governments can set up a supervisory body responsible for monitoring the measures taken and the progress achieved in establishing or developing the teaching of regional or minority languages. Periodic reports can be drawn up, which should be made public.

---

1. Council of Europe, European Charter for Regional or Minority Languages. Explanatory report Strasbourg, 1992).

In order to avoid that the teaching of regional or minority languages become isolated from their historical and cultural context, governments can make arrangements to ensure the teaching of the history and culture of these languages. Regional and minority languages are often part of a separate history and specific traditions and have developed alongside the culture and language of country as a whole. It is desirable that also non-speakers of these languages have access to them. When countries promote their national culture abroad, presentations on regional and minority languages and culture should be included.

Governments have the power or can play an important role in promoting accessibility and a wider use of regional or minority languages. Governments can promote the use of regional and minority languages in cultural activities and facilities, such as (video) libraries, cultural centres, museums, archives, academies, theatres, cinemas, literary work, film productions, vernacular forms of cultural expressions, festivals and cultural industries. Furthermore, governments can financially support translations and post-synchronisation and subtitling activities. Bodies that are responsible for organising cultural activities should be encouraged to recruit staff who have full command of the regional or minority language and strive for direct participation of the users of such languages in the planning of cultural activities. Finally, governments can encourage and support the creation of a body that is responsible for collecting, keeping a copy of and publishing works produced in a regional or minority language.

The question of language is treated differently when it concerns the mother tongue of immigrants. The question is whether immigrants can claim the same language rights as persons belonging to certain regional groups or national minorities. Most governments are of the opinion that immigrant language issues deserve to be addressed separately from those of minorities and, if appropriate, through a specific legal instrument. The recognition of the language of (long-established) immigrant as an official language is usually not favourably considered. In many countries, governments provide translation services, for example, as a temporary arrangement in education and health care institutions.

It is extremely important that immigrants and minorities learn the official language or languages of the country in which they settle themselves. Without language proficiency they will not succeed in participating fully in the political, socio-economic and cultural life of society. Therefore, government, private organisations and the immigrants invest, to their benefit, in language training.

Older countries of immigration have made and continue to make available considerable resources for the learning and teaching of the national language, through the development of curricula, teaching materials, tests and attainment targets for second-language education. Educational programmes are often tailored to the specific needs of categories of immigrants, such as newcomers and their children, refugees, youngsters, man and women.

Some countries have gone a step further and have introduced instruction in the immigrants' native language and culture. This type of instruction was initially aimed at assisting returning migrants to re-integrate in their country of origin. Migrants became immigrants and mother tongue or home language teaching was seen as a means to bridge the cap between the language spoken at the immigrants' home and in society. This would enhance the possibilities to integrate into the host society. In some countries the instruction in the immigrants language and culture has become part of cultural policies. The language and culture of immigrants are regarded as valuable contributions to cultural pluralism. From an economic perspective such instruction is favoured because multilingual staff facilitates access to other countries and markets.

Some languages of immigrants are more widely spoken in Europe than some regional or minority languages. Governments may therefore consider adopting policies along the lines of those applied to regional or minority languages.

Culture and neighbourhoods

The enormous variety of cultures in cities is to a great extent the result of migration. Migration had a tremendous impact on the life of European cities. Cities have grown in population because of internal and international migration. They have lost people who exchanged the inner cities for suburban areas; among them are settled and successful immigrants whose place was taken by newcomers. Cities will continue to attract new migrants who are fulfilling certain jobs in the dynamic and ever changing landscape of cities. Cities are competitors at the global market place. They must make sure that people, business and capital stay and that new people, new business and new capital is attracted.

Many cities have gone through or are still undergoing fundamental changes and as a result urban neighbourhoods take on new importance. Cultural policies are an effective part of policies to bring new life to cities, to regenerate run down neighbourhoods and to create city spirit in dead urban peripheries.[1] Cultural action at the neighbourhood level shapes individual and collective identities and defines the inhabitants' relationship with the city and the world. Culture strengthens people's link to neighbourhoods and builds space-bound collective and individual identities.

---

1. Based on the project of the Council for Cultural Co-operation *Culture and neighbourhoods*. The results of this project are summarised in four publications (Strasbourg, 1998).

Neighbourhoods are not any longer culturally homogeneous and the nature of proximity, the cornerstone of a neighbourhood, is changing. Within one neighbourhood people with different cultural and ethnic backgrounds are living together and are interacting. Neighbourhoods are integrated into the urban transportation system, its inhabitants develop long-distance relationships and they travel on the information highways. Proximity is rediscovered as a major means of counterbalancing impersonality of non-space based metropolitan relationships. Cultural action at the neighbourhood level is building the bridge between face-to-face experiences and the information world or virtual reality. It also can build bridges between ethnically and culturally diverse groups and mediate between them when they compete for scares social and cultural facilities.

During the last twenty-five years there has been an enormous increase in cultural life in European cities. Culture has become a strategic factor in bettering the cities' overall performance. Various strategies are followed, such as the creation or upgrading of cultural facilities and infrastructure (libraries, museums, etc.), the production of cultural events, the assignments of new meanings and functions to public space, rehabilitation of architectural heritage. There are good examples of the inclusion of immigrant and minority cultures in these kinds of programmes. However, still a lot needs to be done to open these programmes for immigrants and minorities and to make these groups participate on an equal footing.

Direct participation in cultural events and activities, rather than simply consumption, contributes to social cohesion. Shared artistic events can help the various groups to actually engage in an intercultural activity. In cases where there is mutual ignorance, contempt or aggression, or even violence, joined activities can bring about dialogue and acceptance. Artistic activities often lead to reflections on the situation in neighbourhoods and cities and subsequently lead to concrete action to improve the situation. National and local governments often ignore or belittle such grass roots activities, instead of encouraging and supporting them.

7.6 Religious diversity

Europe is a diverse continent also in terms of religion. The dominant Christian faith produced diverse denominations – Roman Catholic, Orthodox and Protestant. In certain parts of Europe Islam remained the dominant religion and there are Jewish communities in most European countries. As a result of recent immigration the presence of the Islam has become more visible and other faith communities, such as Hindus, Sikhs and Buddhists, have established themselves in Europe.

This development coincides with increasing secularisation in north, west and south Europe and the renewed attention for religion in east Europe. In some parts of Europe secularisation is accompanied by privatisation and individu-alisation of religion and by the weakening of the churches' social influence. In some instances this leads to a situation where government and public opinion are reluctant to recognise that religion can play a significant and sometimes central role in the life of some immigrant communities. In other parts of Europe churches are regaining their position in society, which was taken from them by communist regimes. In some instances these churches become staunch defenders of national values that are phrased in religious terms. It sometimes leads to chauvinism and intolerance towards other reli-gions and those who confess them. In all parts of Europe there are examples of conflicts based on or fuelled by religion.

Under the Convention on Human Rights everyone has the freedom of thought, conscience and religion. This includes, without discrimination among religions, freedom to manifest religion in worship, teaching, practice and observance. This principle requires translation into concrete policies[1]. Authorities should inform religious minorities and the leaders of their organ-isations of the rights guaranteed by law and sources of funding for particu-lar religious and educational activities.

Realistic assessments, based on a diversity of sources, of numbers of adher-ents of religious communities and organisations are necessary to assist governments and other agencies in the effective implementation of their policies. Where there is a religious presence in the public space (e.g. prayer rooms at airports, burial facilities, road signposting to churches, etc.) all reli-gions should have access to similar facilities. Publicly funded and publicly accessible institutions should reflect the cultural and religious plurality of the population through equality of opportunity and equality of access to resources, as for example, multi-religious chaplainries in prisons and hospi-tals. Health and social services in particular must be sensitive to the specific expectations of cultural and religious communities, especially relating to women's needs. Respect should be had to the outer manifestations of reli-gion, such as dress, dietary requirements and food labelling.

Measures are required to broaden knowledge and strengthen awareness of religious communities and religious pluralism. Schools and education systems should include education about religions in the curriculum. Teaching materi-als on religion across the curriculum should be true to the religion being por-trayed. Public authorities should use all appropriate means to promote a positive and inclusive image of religious communities through policy state-ments, government public relations and media policy. The continuing train-ing of public officials, including teachers and religious personnel at all levels

---

1. The following four paragraphs are based on Group of Consultants on Religious and Cultural Aspects of Equality of Opportunities for Immigrants (Strasbourg, 1995) and on the Seminar on Religion and the integration of immigrants (Strasbourg, 1998).

should aim to make them aware of the religious dimension of integration and the concerns of religious communities.

The religious communities should be encouraged, and where possible supported, to develop their own religious instruction and to inform their members about the functioning of society at large and its institutions and political processes. Government and the judiciary should develop a greater awareness for patterns of religious discrimination. Often the building of places of worship is prevented or unacceptably delayed and public funding for religious organisations denied.

In some countries structures for multi-faith dialogue have been set up. Such a dialogue can improve mutual awareness, understanding and respect. Governments are encouraged to be accessible to dialogue with religious communities at local and national levels and in particular in such sectors as education, planning, health, social welfare, recreation, law and order, etc. A dialogue between governments and religious communities is a constructive forum in which to face the issues of the dependence of certain groups on foreign governments. Alternatives to such dependence might include tax concessions for charitable or religious activity and training on a par with treatment of established religions. Encouraging a dialogue with particular economic and professional sectors will improve understanding and awareness of religious concerns. This is especially urgent in relation to the mass media.

Majority and minority religious communities should be encouraged to contribute to the debates on the fundamental changes which societies are undergoing and the implications for the fundamental values that are holding societies together. Certain elements or manifestations of the religion of immigrants and minorities are perceived as undermining democratic and pluralist societies. Examples are opposite views on the separation between church or religious institutions and the state or state institutions (for example, education), the relationship between civil law and religious law, the role of women in private and public life, participation in the labour market, military or education and dress requirements, etc. Diverse societies are in need of an ongoing debate on such issues. In these debates central values will evolve and become inclusive which increases the possibilities for their wide acceptance. In order to promote cohesion, majority and minority religious organisations should combat certain tendencies in religions, which promote intolerance towards other religions or beliefs and do not respect democratic values and fundamental human rights.

7.7 Family life

Since families play an important role in the promotion of social cohesion, governmental policies should foster the stability of the family life of immigrants. Family reunion schemes should not be too restrictive and include spouse, dependent children and relatives in the ascending line. The waiting period shall not exceed one year. Spouses should obtain, within a reasonable period of time, an independent residence permit and access to the labour market. Visa regimes should not hamper family visits and the occasional returns of the immigrants to their country of origin[1].

Immigrant family life changes dramatically as a result of migration. Faced with an entirely new situation, both immigrant men and women are confronted with different expectations with regard to their roles as husband and wife. Men and women need to be given time to adapt themselves to the new situation and in that process, children play an important role as builders of bridges between the country of origin culture and that of the society in which they live. Greater recognition should be given to the fact that immigrants' identities are built within the family that remains a source of support and solidarity, especially in times of conflict.

The family life of immigrants and minorities may differ considerably from that of the majority. In many countries, these differences provoke debates on the limits of diversity. The question that arises is to what extent a certain immigrant or minority's right to act according to their own standards is limited by human right standards that prevail in society. There are a number of clear-cut cases where the values and practices, for example, female genital mutilation, of certain immigrants and minorities conflict with accepted and universal human rights. The situation is much more complex in cases such as the wearing of headscarves. This is seen by some as oppression of women and by others as an expression of cultural diversity. In these cases, much more dialogue is needed in order to understand the differences in family life between minorities and the majority before such differences are condemned as violations of human rights or the principles of a state.

Immigrant women deserve special attention of governments and non-governmental actors. They share with other women problems related to the position of women in modern society. Family commitments and expectations often prevent women, irrespective of their national or ethnic origin, from actively participating in the wider society. In addition, immigrant women are facing problems related to their position as immigrant women. In some instances the culture of some immigrant communities resists their participation in society. This adds to the obstacles the host society puts on their way to full participation. Immigrant women are often victims of double discrimination, namely on the basis of gender and ethnic origin or skin colour.

In many European countries governments are taking measures aiming to combat gender discrimination and to promote equality of treatment for men

---

1. The following paragraphs in this section are based on the Council of Europe's publication *Immigrant women and integration* (Strasbourg, 1995) and the Joint Specialist Group on Migration, Cultural Diversity and Equality of Women and Men, Final Report of Activities (Strasbourg, 1996).

and women. Barriers to equal access to education and participation in the labour market are being removed. Public and private services (such as health care) are adjusted so that they also respond to the needs of women. Considerable progress has been made in these areas from which also immigrant women have benefited. For example, many immigrant women have established themselves as entrepreneurs or successfully entered the labour market. Immigrant women could benefit even more from a general gender policy when governments and non-governmental actors include immigrant women in its design and adopt a strategy of reaching out to the immigrant communities. Such an approach could effectively tackle double discrimination.

Immigrant women are confronted with problems that are related to their position as immigrant women. Specific measures need to be taken to address these problems, in particular in the following fields: literacy and learning the host country's language, vocational training, health and cultural action.

Literacy and language programmes ensure that immigrant women become gradually accustomed to the host society. Women mediators from the same background can help to build immigrant women's confidence. Teaching programmes should initially give priority to the spoken language and conversation. The contents and teaching methods need to be adapted to the specific situation of immigrant women. The language courses need to be combined with a wider understanding of family life, health, social customs, working life and the laws and institutions of the host society. Childcare arrangements would enable immigrant women to attend language courses.

Special measures need to be taken to provide vocational training to immigrant women who often lack professional qualifications. Such training familiarise immigrant women with the constraints of working life and visits to firms facilitates the acceptance of the idea of women pursuing a professional career. Women often have professional qualifications that are acquired in the country of origin. These qualifications are not always recognised or valued by employers (which asks for a change of their attitudes), or are not meeting the labour requirements of the host society (which asks for courses which compliment the qualifications immigrant women already have).

The physical and psychological health problems of immigrant women need to be addressed as well. First generation immigrant women often find themselves deprived from traditional family networks in the country of origin and live an isolated life in the host country. They have to fulfil the same functions in the family as in the host country but without its support network. This may lead to lose of self-respect and mental and physical health problem. The language problem often prevents real communication with doctors and other medical staff. Gynaecological and family planning clinics need to pay special attention to immigrant women. More than is the case in such areas as language training and education, it is essential to have women mediators from the same background and to train health care personnel.

Cultural expression enhances immigrant women's image. Drama groups, choirs, making newspapers or television programmes demonstrate immigrant women's creativity. These activities encourage communication with people from different backgrounds, help to motivate women to participate in society and give them self-confidence. Activities organised to make immigrant women familiar with the host country's cultural heritage have the double effect of making this heritage more accessible and becoming a shared heritage.

7.8 Media

Digitalisation and the convergence of mass communication, telecommunication and computers are shaping the modern information society. There are infinitely more opportunities for individuals and groups to communicate and to exchange information then ever before. The modern media are, therefore, crucial for the exchanges and dialogue between cultures. They can also foster the particular identity of immigrant communities and minorities. Immigrants, for example, maintain links with their country and culture of (distant) origin through satellite television and other forms of modern communication. Access to modern mass media is crucial for minorities when they want to preserve their own identity.

Governments are recommended to adopt a positive action approach in order to achieve pluralism in the media. Public service broadcasting plays its own vital role and can guarantee pluralistic communication that is accessible for everyone. In addition, measures are needed to limit the effects of market principles or monopolistic tendencies in the media and to promote fair competition[1].

Governments are recommended to ensure or encourage the creation of at least one radio station and one television channel in the regional or minority languages. Governments can also facilitate the production and distribution of newspapers and audio-visual works in the regional or minority languages, or encourage other organisations to do so. The additional costs for media that use regional or minority languages can be covered by governments when the law provides for financial assistance in general for media. Governments can also support the training of journalists and other staff for media using regional or minority languages. The interest of users of these languages should be represented within bodies that are responsible for guaranteeing the freedom and pluralism of the media. The authorities should also guarantee freedom of direct reception of radio and television broadcasts from neighbouring countries. No restrictions will be placed on the freedom of expression and free circulation of information in the written press. These provisions can also be applied to the media of immigrants.

---

1. 4th European Ministers Conference on Mass Media Policy (Prague, 1994).

In cases where they provide means for the education of journalists, governments are recommended to make sure that access criteria do not favour persons belonging to the majority at the detriment of immigrants and minorities and that teachers are recruited among these communities. Tolerance and anti-racism need to be included in student courses and professional standards need to be developed on how to deal with racism in society. In addition, journalists and media professionals should be engaged in ongoing exchanges with immigrants and minorities and with experts working with them.

With the liberalisation of the broadcasting sector, regulatory bodies have been created in many European countries. The mandate of such bodies usually includes the promotion of pluralistic information. In their work, these bodies have often neglected immigrant and minority communities. This can be redressed by the incorporation of representatives of these communities in these bodies.

The growing power of the media put heavy responsibilities upon those who own or work for the media, also with regard to the immigrant and minority communities. Self-regulation by way of adopting codes of ethics for journalists and establishing press councils is now quite common in Europe. Usually, the codes of ethics and the press councils have banned open forms of racism and xenophobia in the media, but little has been done to promote a fair and accurate portrayal of immigrants and minorities in the media. Some media, broadcast and journalists organisations have launched a prize for tolerance in journalism. The Council of Europe and the EU Commission support this initiative. The award aims to raise awareness among journalists and media professionals of their role in countering racism, xenophobia, anti-Semitism and intolerance. The Prize also seeks to promote investigative work that encourages a better understanding between people of different ethnic and cultural backgrounds.

Freedom of expression constitutes one of the essential foundations of a democratic and diverse society and one of the basic conditions for its progress and for individual's self-fulfilment. Freedom of expression offers the opportunity to take part in the public exchange of cultural, political and social information and ideas of all kinds. Article 10 of the Convention on Human Rights guarantees the right of freedom of expression for everyone, including immigrants and minorities. The right includes holding opinions and receiving and disseminating information and ideas without interference by public authorities and regardless frontiers. This freedom is, however, not an absolute, but is subject to certain restrictions as are described by law and are necessary in a democratic society. These restrictions, which apply to everyone, including immigrants and minorities, cover the protection of health and morals and the reputation or rights of other persons. On several occasions the European Commission on Human Rights decided that the freedom of expression may not be invoked in a sense contrary to the rights and freedoms set forth in the Convention. For example, the publication of materials inciting racial discrimination and hatred cannot be defended on the basis of article 10 of the Human Rights Convention. In this way restrictions on freedom of expression contribute to cohesion.

A number of member states have made punishable by criminal law incitement to discrimination, hatred or violence towards persons because of race, colour, descent or national or ethnic origin. The observance of these laws requires an active role of the judicial authorities. In this area there is still room for improvement. The staff of judicial authorities should receive training, which make them more aware of open and covert forms of racism in the media. Special offices within judicial authorities could be established or special staff appointed to combat racism in the media.

7.9 Tackling racism and intolerance

The elimination of all forms of racial discrimination is essential for democratic societies. Most member states rely on constitutional clauses prohibiting racial discrimination, but only a limited number have bolstered such protection through the introduction of anti-discrimination legislation. Numerous initiatives have been taken which aimed at promoting tolerance and combating racism, at the local, regional, national and international level. The persistence of racial discrimination in European societies – in both urban and rural areas and between immigrant and minority groups – calls for continuous governmental and non-governmental action at all levels.

Racial and ethnic discrimination cannot be eliminated by legal measures alone, but legal measures are nevertheless of paramount importance. National criminal, civil and administrative law should expressly and specifically counter racism, *inter alia* by providing that discrimination in employment and in the supply of goods and services is unlawful. Furthermore, racist acts are stringently punished through methods such as defining common offences but with a racist nature as specific offences, enabling the racist motives of the offender to be specifically taken into account. Oral, written, audio-visual, electronic and other forms of expressions inciting to hatred, discrimination or violence against immigrants and minorities should be legally categorised as a criminal offence. This should also cover the production, the distribution and the storage for distribution of such materials Legal measures can be taken to combat racist organisations, including the banning of such organisations[1].

---

1. This and the following two paragraphs are based on the European Commission against Racism and Intolerance General Policy Recommendations No. 1 and No. 2.

Non-enforcement of existing legislation discredits action against racism and intolerance. Governments must therefore ensure that criminal prosecution of offences of a racist or xenophobic nature is given a high priority and is actively and consistently undertaken. Accurate data and statistics should be collected and published on the number of racist and xenophobic offences that are reported to the police, on the number of cases that are prosecuted, on the reasons for not prosecuting and on the outcome of cases prosecuted. Furthermore, adequate legal remedies must be made available to victims of discrimination, either in criminal law or in administrative and civil law where pecuniary or other compensation may be secured. Adequate legal assistance should be is available to victims of discrimination when seeking a legal remedy. Victims of racism need to be informed on the availability of legal remedies and the possibilities of access to them.

Specialised bodies should be set up which aim to combat racism. These bodies should be given terms of reference, which are clearly set out in a constitutional or other legislative text. They should be provided with sufficient funds to carry out their functions effectively and the funding should be subject annually to the approval of parliament. They have the following responsibilities. First, they work towards the elimination of the various forms of discrimination, to promote equality of opportunity and good relations between persons belonging to all the different groups in society. Second, they monitor the content and effect of legislation and executive acts with respect to their relevance to the aim of combating racism. Third, they advise the legislative and executive authorities with a view to improving regulations and practice in the relevant fields. Four, they provide aid and assistance to victims, including legal aid, in order to secure their rights before institutions and the courts. Five, they have recourse to the courts or other judicial authorities as appropriate if and when necessary. Six they hear and consider complaints and petitions concerning specific cases and to seek settlements either through amicable conciliation or, within the limits prescribed by the law, through binding and enforceable decisions. Seven, they have appropriate powers to obtain evidence and information in pursuance of its functions. Eight, they provide information and advice to relevant bodies and institutions, including State bodies and institutions. Nine, they issue advice on standards of anti-discriminatory practice in specific areas which might either have the force of law or be voluntary in their application. Ten, they promote and contribute to the training of certain key groups without prejudice to the primary training role of the professional organisations involved. Eleven, they promote the awareness of the general public to issues of discrimination and to produce and publish pertinent information and documents. Twelve, they support and encourage organisations with similar objectives to those of the specialised body. Thirteen, they take account of and reflect as appropriate the concerns of such organisations.

An important aspect of legislative measures to combat racial discrimination is the review of existing legislation for any discriminatory clauses and articles.

Some countries have completed such a review whereas the majority of member states have yet to start and complete such a review.

Countries with anti-discrimination legislation are looking for ways to improve such legislation and make it more effective in practice. In this respect governments are looking at lessons that can be learnt from legal measures against gender discrimination, in particular with regard to the principles of indirect discrimination and the shift of the burden of proof. These two principles have been introduced by the European Union legislation on gender discrimination. Indirect discrimination pertains to seemingly neutral provisions, criteria or practices that disproportionately disadvantage persons of particular racial or ethnic background, where this cannot be justified by objective factors. The shift of the burden of proof means that not the victims of racism have to prove that discrimination has occurred, but perpetrator must prove that discrimination has not occurred. Victims have to establish before a court or another competent body facts from which may be presumed that there has been direct or indirect discrimination.

In co-operation with non-governmental actors, governments can adopt anti-racist policies in a number of areas. Measures in the fields of education and information can strengthen the fight against all forms of racial discrimination. They include measures that enhance the awareness of the richness that cultural diversity brings to society. School curricula, particularly in the field of teaching history, can be set up in such a way to enhance the appreciation of cultural diversity. Research can be undertaken into the nature, causes and manifestations of racial discrimination. Training courses can be developed which promote cultural sensitivity, awareness of prejudice and knowledge of legal aspects of discrimination. These courses could be given to those responsible for recruitment and promotion procedures, for those who have direct contact with the public and for those responsible for ensuring that persons in the organisation comply with standards and policies of non-discrimination and equal opportunity. Such training should in particular be introduced and maintained for policy personnel and criminal justice agencies. The police should provide equal treatment to all members of the public and avoid any act of racism, xenophobia, anti-Semitism and intolerance. Formal and informal structures for dialogue can be established between the police and immigrant and minority communities, and a mechanism can be created for independent enquiry into incidents and areas of conflicts between the police and minority groups. The recruitment must be encouraged of members of public services, and in particular police and support staff, from minority groups. All public services and services of a public nature such as healthcare, social services and education must provide non-discriminatory access to all members of the public. Specific measures, such as providing targeted information, must ensure that all eligible groups de facto have equal access to these services. Research needs to be done into discriminatory practices and barriers or exclusionary mechanisms in public and private sector housing; Governments must ensure that public sector housing is allocated on the basis of published criteria that are justifiable, i.e. which ensure equal access to all those eligible, irrespective of ethnic origin[1].

7.10 Political participation[2]

There are significant differences within Europe in the way immigrant and minority issues are perceived and defined, and these differences are reflected in consultation structures and mechanisms. Special consultative arrangements, at the local, regional and national levels, may be justified not only on the basis of immigrant status or immigrant origin, but also on the basis of national or ethnic origin, religion, culture, language, race, foreign citizenship, refugee status or any combination of these. In several European countries, special structures exist for dialogue between national minorities. There are also systems of official representation of national minorities in national or regional parliaments. Furthermore, trans-frontier co-operation also enhances participation of national minorities in decision-making structures.

A distinction can be made between individual and group participation of immigrants. The former includes naturalisation as well as the granting of voting rights to non-citizens. In situations where the immigrants' share in the population is increasing, the public and policy debates on naturalisation and voting rights tend to be intensified. In some cases these debates lead to the adoption of measures facilitating naturalisation and dual nationality. In other cases the debates lead to granting voting rights at local level to immigrants. Nationals of EU member states have, in whatever member state they live, the right to vote and stand for election in local and European elections. Extension of this right to immigrants from outside the European Union is in some member states already a fact, in some others under discussion and in again some others rejected.

Political parties should encourage the participation of immigrants and minorities not only in elections, but also in the life of the party. Immigrants and minorities should be recruited within the ranks of political parties and selected as candidates in elections. During election time, special efforts should be made to reach out to the immigrant and minority communities through information campaigns that highlight the importance of electoral participation. Such campaigns must address issues of concern to immigrants and minorities

Consultation is a form of group participation. It may take place in a formalised and well-structured manner, although informal consultation can also

---

1. This paragraph is based on European Commission against Racism and Intolerance's General Policy Recommendations No. 1.
2. Based on the Conclusions of the seminar on "Political and Social Participation of Immigrants through Consultative Bodies" (Strasbourg, 1997).

be quite effective. Both forms do not exclude each another, but they can be complementary. Similarly, consultation should never serve as a substitute for gradually granting to immigrants the same rights as the majority population enjoys. Consultation mechanisms should not be set up in times of crisis, but at a much earlier stage, precisely to help avoid such crises. Consultative bodies should have a formal basis and there should be agreement on their tasks and aims. They should be equipped with sufficient staff and funding, so as to enable them to be professional and serious partners in the debate. They have a practical as well as an important symbolic value, namely as signal that immigrants and minorities are taken seriously. This is particularly the case if such bodies have direct access to high-level politicians and to the media.

The need of consultation at an early stage of the decision-making process is important. This makes consultative bodies into real participants in the decision-making processes and reduces the chance that they serve as a legitimisation for decisions already taken. Consultative bodies should primarily express themselves on issues that are of direct relevance for the immigrant and minority communities.

The members of consultative bodies could include not only representatives of immigrants or minorities, but also representatives of political or administrative bodies and other relevant institutions. Another option is that membership is reserved for immigrants and minority associations, who could then engage in a dialogue as equal partners with the authorities. The effectiveness of either approach seems to be largely dependent on the national situation and traditions. Consultative bodies should always be seen as supplementary to normal parliamentary procedures and never as an alternative.

Significant differences exist between the European countries regarding membership and recruitment practices for consultative bodies. In some cases immigrant members of these bodies are 'well connected' individuals who only represent themselves. In other cases the immigrant members may be representatives of one particular (national) group, in again other cases immigrant members may represent the entire immigrant community. In the latter two cases immigrant members are sometimes elected, e.g. from among immigrant associations. There are other situations where immigrant members of consultative bodies are appointed, usually by the government.

It is very important for members of consultative bodies to act as mediators between immigrant communities and the authorities, and, therefore, to have the confidence of both sides. This implies that the members should have a good knowledge of the varying position and situation of immigrants and minorities. The diversity between as well as within immigrant and minority groups should be sufficiently reflected in their representation, and should be gender balanced.

Chapter VIII: Monitoring and measuring

This chapter explores how the implementation of policies can be monitored and their results measured. It looks mainly at the evaluation and results assessment of governmental policies although some of the principles and practices could also apply to non-governmental actors.

Monitoring

The monitoring of the implementation of governmental policies and the involvement thereby of both official institutions and non-governmental actors enhance the effectiveness and credibility of policies. In addition, applying human rights standards requires continuous monitoring and the exposure of violations of the rights of immigrants and minorities.

Monitoring is only possible when policies are transparent at all stages, from formation to implementation. Transparent practices of member states vary considerably due to different traditions of openness of governmental decision making processes and access to official documents.

The executive branch of government is accountable and has to report to national and regional parliaments and municipal councils. Self-governments of minorities (i.e., immigrant and other ethnic associations) are held accountable to minority communities. Governments can decide to hold regular debates on immigrant and minority policies, which would allow for the review of all aspects of governmental policies in those areas and link them to broader issues of diversity and cohesion. Regular debates would ensure that these issues are not solely discussed when problems arise or during election times.

National and regional parliamentary agendas, and those of municipal councils, in addition to policy papers and legislative proposals, need to be accessible to the press and the public. Parliamentary and municipal meetings, in principle, are open to the press and public, allowing them to attend or otherwise follow official debates. Reports of those meetings should be made available on a wide scale.

In many countries, national and local governments have established official or semi-official institutions to implement (or oversee the implementation of) policies in the areas of human rights, immigration, minorities, anti-discrimination and equality. In some instances, these organisations are also authorised to receive complaints from (groups of) individual citizens and to propose solutions to those complaints. Among such organisations are human rights commissions, offices of the ombudsman and (race) equality commissions.

Reports from such organisations are valuable indicators of the effective implementation of governmental policies.

In order to be kept informed on how policies work in practice, governments could establish a structured dialogue with immigrant and minority organisations and other interested parties. This could take various forms, from the creation of consultative commissions to consultations on specific issues.

Laws and regulations concerning residence rights, equal treatment, anti-discrimination and nationality must be observed. The judiciary plays an essential role in monitoring the observance of law by governmental and non-governmental actors and individual citizens. There are also examples of the appointment of special public prosecutors and judges responsible for matters related to human rights violations, discrimination and racism.

Non-governmental actors also play an important role in monitoring the implementation of governmental policies. Academic research may provide governments with scientific information on how policies are implemented and which factors present obstacles for further policy implementation. Governments can also draw lessons from the experiences of trade unions and employers organisations when these social partners implement specific legislation or other measures. Immigrant and minority associations and other non-governmental organisations are often among the first to point out the failed implementation of declared governmental policies, as well as the first to signal and denounce human rights violations.

The situation is more or less the same at the level of the Council of Europe and the European Union. Although they do not have the same power as national parliaments, the Council of Europe's Parliamentary Assembly and the European Union's European Parliament oversee the policies and activities of the Council of Europe and the European Union, respectively. The European Court of Human Rights and the European Court of Justice monitor the observance of the European Human Rights Convention and Community law, respectively. There also exist international organisations that oversee the implementation of certain policies (for example, the European Monitoring Centre on Racism and Xenophobia). Finally, international organisations of non-governmental actors play a similar role at the European level as they do at the national level.

European conventions and their supervisory mechanisms are also important monitoring instruments. State parties are obliged to report regularly on the implementation of these conventions. Governments could involve non-governmental actors in the writing of these national reports, which should also be made available to the public. National reports are submitted to treaty bodies (designated under the conventions to assess the national reports) that, on the basis thereof, draft reports on the implementation of conventions in the countries concerned. This report may contain recommendations as to how to improve the implementation of the conventions. The treaty bodies are usually composed of independent experts appointed by governments and, in some instances, include non-governmental actors. Their powers differ under the various conventions, and their reports and recommendations are not usually binding for the concerned countries. Nevertheless, they carry a strong political message to bring national policies in line with international standards.

An additional and less legalistic method to assess policy implementation is the organisation of round tables (such as those organised by the Committee on Migration) and country-by country reporting (as is practised by the European Commission against Racism and Intolerance). Such instruments assist governments in incorporating international standards into national law and practices.

Policies and practices of non-governmental actors should also be monitored. Employers, for example, could apply equal treatment measures by establishing targets for the numbers of immigrants and minorities to be recruited and promoted. Internal or external audits could be established to monitor the implementation of such measures. Similarly, trade unions and employers organisations may work together to combat racism on the shop floor and to establish internal mechanisms to monitor the implementation of anti-discrimination measures.

Measuring[1]

An important complement to monitoring policy implementation is the ability to measure concrete results. Only by measuring can one assess whether policies and other measures are effective in facilitating inclusion, expanding participation, ending hidden and unfair advantages and promoting diversity.

There are nevertheless a number of complicating factors surrounding measuring. First, there needs to be clarity about what is to be measured. Broad policy concepts need to be directed towards clear policy targets. There may be significant differences between countries, as well as between the various stakeholders within countries, with regards to broad policy concepts and specific policy targets. The involvement of all stakeholders, including immigrants and minorities, is essential in defining these targets. As has been shown in this report, there is considerable agreement on the overall strategies for the integration of immigrants and minorities. They include securing residence rights, equal treatment, naturalisation and anti-discrimination efforts. With these in mind, governments can set a series of targets, for example, to issue permanent residence permits after a limited number of years, reduce the number of unemployed minorities, simplify naturalisation

---

1. This section is also based on *Measurement and indicators of integration* (Council of Europe, 1997)

procedures, and adopt anti-discrimination clauses in civil and penal laws. The development of policy targets naturally leads to definitions of "integration indicators". Similarly, diversity indicators can be developed, for example, educational and health services must target diverse populations and be responsive to their diverse needs. A list of those needs and what it takes to respond to them can be translated into "diversity indicators".

Second, there must be an agreement on the methods of measuring. Those individuals who are directly concerned need to be involved in whichever method adopted. Quantitative and qualitative methods can be applied either alternatively or in combination. Population censuses often include information on education, occupation, employment status, languages spoken, national or ethnic origin. This provides a wealth of information on the composition of the population, demographic trends, changes in the labour market position, etc. Analysis of the data may provide insights into the number of foreigners and immigrants, the naturalisation rates, the number of mixed marriages, the fertility rates of immigrants as compared to other groups, the level of education, the employment status, etc. Periodic surveys of households may give additional and more in-depth information on these issues. Longitudinal research on processes of immigrant integration or diversifying labour pools provides valuable information on the successes and failures of integration and diversity policies. Qualitative surveys can assess, for example, the acceptance of immigrants and minorities (so-called "barometers"), the added value of diversity management, etc.

Third, for various historical experiences and/or national traditions, a significant number of European countries remain averse to registration of ethnic origin or belonging to an ethnic group. Consequently, naturalised immigrants and minorities do not appear in statistics. This hampers the measurement of the employment status of minorities (recruitment, retention and promotion), participation of minorities in the labour market and school performances, to name only a few examples.

Notwithstanding these difficulties, measuring can serve as an important tool to enhance the effectiveness of policies and to detect and remove barriers for the full participation of immigrants and minorities in society. The following list of indicators of integration and diversity can be developed and used.

Secure residence status enhances integration. The list of indicators related to this issue includes:

- Waiting periods and number of conditions for acquiring permanent residence status
- Numbers of issued permanent residence permits per annum
- Accompanying entitlements (access to labour market, freedom of movement, etc.)
- Length of the validity of the status and procedures to extend the permit

– Annual numbers of family members united with their families
– Waiting periods and criteria for family reunion
– Number of grounds of expulsion
– Number of expulsions per annum

Qualitative surveys may provide information on the sense of security among the immigrant and minority population.

Equal treatment is the cornerstone of European integration policies. The list of indicators includes the following items (and also distinguishes by age and gender):

1. *Demographic aspects:*
   – nationality
   – sex
   – age bracket 0-6/6-12/12-18/18-25/25-45/45-65/+65
   – birth/fertility rates

2. *Type of immigration:*
   – family reunion
   – refugees
   – marriage
   – economic immigration
   – number of expulsions

3. *Inclusion in the labour market*

   a. *Activity sector*
   – primary
   – secondary
   – tertiary

   Public/private sector

   b. *Status*
   – none
   – short-term, long-term unemployed
   – semi-skilled, skilled worker
   – lower level, higher-level white-collar worker
   – manager
   – self-employed, small business
   – independent professions
   – manager of a business 0-10 persons; > 10 persons

4. *Employment – training*

   a. *level of qualifications*
   – none
   – primary school
   – lower secondary school
   – upper secondary school

                              – diploma level
                              – university level

  b. *participation and number of hours*

                              – in vocational training
                              – in continuing education and training for social advancement
                              – literacy and language courses
                              – unionisation of seasonal workers

5. *Social benefits*

                              – registered for social security
                              – family allowance beneficiaries
                              – pension beneficiaries
                              – health insurance beneficiaries
                              – more than 66% disability
                              – beneficiary of minimum subsistence allowance

6. *Housing*

  – type of housing   – single family house
                              – flat
                              – studio or room

  – status of housing   – owner
                              – private tenant
                              – low-cost housing tenant

  – quality of housing   – with individual bathroom
                              – with central heating
                              – $< 20m^2$; $> 20m^2$ per person

  – housing environment   – low-cost housing neighbourhood
                              – urban neighbourhood
                              – suburbvrural area

7. *Education*

  participation in   – pre-schooling
                              – primary school
                              – lower secondary school
                              – upper secondary school
                              – vocational school
                              – diploma level
                              – university level
                              – training for social advancement
                              – vocational training for adults
                              – continuing education

8. *Participation in social, political and cultural life*

- rate of participation in local voluntary organisations
- rate of participation in social organisations
- trade unions
- mutual benefit society
- low-cost housing
- employer organisationsvschool boards
- rate of participation in political parties
- rate of voter registrationvrate of partici-pation in European, national, regional, local electionsvproportion of immigrant candidates
- proportion of immigrant elected repre-sentativesvrate of participation in key institutions or bodies

There are often legal barriers to equal treatment and participation in specific areas of public life. A list of these barriers could be drafted, and qualitative research could provide information on whether immigrants and minorities feel that they are treated equally.

Naturalisation facilitates integration. Indicators are:

- Conditions and waiting periods for the acquisition of nationality

- Possibilities for dual nationality

- Naturalisation rates among the various categories of immigrants or mino-rities

Qualitative surveys may provide information on the sense of belonging to a country among the immigrant and minority population.

Indicators on discrimination and racism are:

- Data on racist and discriminatory acts

- Data on racially violent crimes and racial harassment

- Numbers of complaints of discrimination and convictions

- Data on discriminatory patterns in governmental offices (including the police)

- Data on direct and indirect discriminatory patterns in the private sector (labour market and services)

These data should be supplemented by data on attitudes, opinions and per-ceptions. In addition to surveys of the general population, targeted surveys should be developed, which ascertain the experiences and perceptions of (potential) victims of racism.

The costs of discrimination are also high in economic terms, for instance, the costs of excluding highly skilled immigrants and minorities from the labour market. Indicators can be developed to measure these costs.

With regard to diversity, a list of indicators can be developed for the respective spheres of public life, the economy, education, culture, etc. To some extent, these indicators will be an elaboration of the indicators on equal treatment and anti-discrimination.

Indicators can be developed on the visibility of immigrants and minorities in public life. The staff of governmental offices ought to reflect the overall population. Assessments can be made of recruitment, professional training and promotion of immigrants and minorities. Governmental service providers should adapt their services to serve a diverse population. Inventories of these needs can be taken, as well as accompanying targets for addressing these needs. After a specified period of time, assessments can be made of the effectiveness of measures applied to achieve these targets.

Similar measures can be taken by the private sector. Inventories of corporate mission statements expressing their intention to be equal opportunity employers and to employ a diverse work force can also be conducted. In addition, indicators can be developed to assess changes in company culture. Equally, the increase or decrease in output can be measured and linked to a company's diversity management. These methods can also apply to government employers.

Media can be screened on articles and programmes devoted to diversity issues and the visibility of immigrant and minority staff.

Finally, another diversity indicator is the amount of governmental subsidies or private sector sponsorship made available for the promotion of immigrant and minority culture and arts.

Annex I

Migratory movements in Europe

Table 1
Components of population changes in Europe, 1995-98

		annual average per cent		
		Groth rate	Natural increase	Net migration
Albania	[1]	–	–	–
Andorra		0,13	0,77	−0,64
Austria		0,12	0,07	0,06
Belgium		0,20	0,10	0,
Bulgaria	[5]	−0,59	−0,59	0,01
Croatia	[2]	−0,64	0,05	−0,68
Cyprus		0,73	0,66	0,07
Czech Republic		−0,11	−0,21	0,10
Denmark		0,46	0,14	0,33
Estonia		−0,78	−0,45	−0,34
Finland		0,30	0,21	0,09
France		0,40	0,34	0,07
Germany		0,15	−0,10	0,25
Greece		0,21	0,01	0,21
Hungary		−0,38	−0,38	0,00
Iceland		0,79	0,88	−0,09
Ireland	[2]	0,88	0,51	0,37
Italy		0,15	−0,05	0,20
Latvia		−0,91	−0,63	−0,28
Liechtenstein	[1]	1,11	0,61	0,23
Lithuania		−0,11	−0,10	−0,01
Luxembourg		1,35	0,39	0,97
Malta	[3]	0,58	0,49	0,09
Moldova		−0,32	−0,04	−0,28
Netherlands		0,54	0,36	0,18
Norway		0,55	0,35	0,20
Poland		0,06	0,09	−0,04
Portugal		0,17	0,06	0,11
Romania		−0,25	−0,18	−0,07

Russian Federation	−0,27	−0,52	0,25
San Marino	1,50	0,36	1,14
Slovak Republic	0,17	0,14	0,04
Slovenia	−0,14	−0,02	−0,12
Spain	0,14	0,03	0,11
Sweden	0,11	0,01	0,10
Switzerland	0,34	0,26	0,08
"the Former Yougoslav Republic of Madedonia" [2]	0,76	0,74	0,02
Turkey	1,40	1,57	−0,06
Ukraine [4]	−0,77	...	0,77
United Kingdom [2]	0,33	0,16	0,18
Armenia	0,30	0,55	−0,26
Azerbaijan	0,98	1,08	−0,10
Belarus	−0,29	−0,39	0,11
Bosnia and Herzegovina	...	...	...
Georgia	...	...	...
Federal Republic of Yugoslavia [2,6]	0,25	0,25	0,00

Source: Council of Europe, 1999, *Recent demographic developments in Europe.*

Notes:
1. 1995-96 average
2. 1995-97 average
3. 1995-96, 98 average
4. 1995 only (growth and net migration only)
5. 1996 only (net migration only)
6. 1997 only (net migration only)

Table 2 – *Stock of foreign polulation in selected European countries,*
1980-1997 (thousands)

A – Western Europe

	1980	1981	1982	1983	1984	1985	1986	1987
Austria[1]	282,7	299,2	302,9	296,7	297,8	304,4	314,9	326,2
Belgium[2]	–	885,7	891,2	890,9	897,6	846,5	853,2	862,5
Denmark[3]	101,6	101,9	103,1	104,1	107,7	117,0	128,3	136,2
Finland[4]	12,8	13,7	14,3	15,7	16,8	17,0	17,3	17,7
France[5]	–	–	3714,2	–	–	3752,2	–	–
Germany[6]	4453,3	4629,8	4666,9	4534,9	4363,7	4378,9	4512,7	4630,2
Greece[7]	213,0	223,0	229,7	232,0	234,1	233,2	220,1	217,8
Ireland[8, 12]	–	–	–	–	–	–	–	–
Italy[9]	298,7	331,7	358,9	381,3	403,9	423,0	450,2	572,1
Luxembourg[16]	94,3	95,4	95,6	96,2	96,9	98,0	96,8	98,6
Netherlands	520,9	537,6	546,5	552,4	558,7	552,5	568,0	591,8
Norway[10]	82,6	86,5	90,6	94,7	97,8	101,5	109,3	123,7
Portugal[11, 12]	49,3	53,6	57,7	65,9	72,6	80,0	87,0	89,8
Spain[12]	182,0	197,9	200,9	210,4	226,5	241,9	293,2	334,9
Swede[13]	421,7	414,0	405,5	397,1	390,6	388,6	390,8	401,0
Switzerland[14]	892,8	909,9	925,8	925,6	932,4	939,7	956,0	978,7
Turkey	–	–	–	–	–	–	24,9	–
United Kingdom[15]	–	–	–	–	1601,0	1731,0	1820,0	1839,0

B – Central and eastern Europe[19]

	1980	1981	1982	1983	1984	1985	1986	1987
Bulgaria[20]	–	–	–	–	–	–	–	–
Czech Republic[21]	–	–	–	–	–	–	–	34,6
Hungary[22]	–	–	–	–	–	–	–	–
Poland[23]	–	–	–	–	–	–	–	–
Romania[24]	–	–	–	–	–	–	–	–
Slovenia[25]	–	–	–	–	–	–	–	–
Russia[26]	–	–	–	–	–	–	–	–
Latvia[27]	–	–	–	–	–	–	–	–

1. 1983 to 1993 data from Sopemi (1994)
2. In 1985, as a consequence of a modification of the nationality code, some persons who formerly would have been counted as foreigners were included as nationals. This led to a marked decrease in the foreign population. Source: Eurostat (1994) and Sopemi (1994)
3. Data for a given year are those of 1/1 following year
4. Source: Central statistical office of Finland.
5. Population censuses on 4/3/82 and 6/3/90. The figure for the census of 20/2/75 is 3442.4
6. Data as of 30/10 up to 1984 and in 1990 and as of 31/12 for all other years. Except for 1991 & 1992, refers to western Germany. FSO.
7. Source: NSSG (1994) and Minsitry of Public Order in 1995 report to the OECD by the Greek SOPEMI Correspondent. 1993 and 1994 figures rounded.
8. Department of Justice, annual returns, (excludes U.K. citizens). 1995 figure from report to OECD from Irish SOPEMI correspondent.
9. Data are adjusted to take account of the regularisations which occurred in 1987-88 and 1990. The fall in numbers for 1989 results from a review of the foreigners' register (removing duplicate registrations, accounting for returns). Source: Ministry of the Interior, elaborated by CENSIS.
10. From 1987, asylum seekers whose requests are being processed are included. Numbers for earlier years were fairly small.
11. Source: Servião de Estrangeiros e Fronteiras. 1993 figure includes estimated 39,200 from special regularisation.
12. Eurostat (1994) and Sopemi (1994)
13. Some foreigners permits of short duration are not counted (mainly citizens of other Nordic countries).

1988	1989	1990	1991	1992	1993	1994[17]	1995[18]	1996	1997
344,0	387,2	456,1	532,7	623,0	689,0	713,5	723,0	728,0	732,7
868,8	880,8	904,5	922,5	909,3	920,6	922,3	909,7	911,9	903,1
142,0	150,6	160,6	169,5	180,1	189,0	196,7	222,7	237,7	237,7
18,7	21,2	26,3	37,6	46,3	55,6	62,0	68,6	73,8	81,0
–	–	3607,6	3596,6	–	–	–	–	–	–
4489,1	4845,9	5241,8	5882,3	6495,8	6878,1	6990,5	7173,9	7314,0	–
222,6	226,1	229,1	253,3	262,3	265,0	244,0	153,0	155,0	–
–	79,3	80,8	87,7	94,9	89,9	91,1	96,1	117,8	114,4
645,4	490,4	781,1	859,6	925,2	987,4	922,7	991,4	1095,6	1240,7
100,9	104,0	110,0	114,7	119,7	124,5	130,0	132,5	138,1	142,8
623,7	641,9	692,4	732,9	757,4	779,8	757,1	728,4	679,9	–
135,9	140,3	143,3	147,8	154,0	162,3	164,0	160,8	157,5	–
94,7	101,0	107,8	114,0	121,5	170,8	157,1	157,0	168,3	172,9
360,0	398,1	407,7	360,7	393,1	430,4	461.0	499,8	539,0	609,8
421,0	456,0	483,7	493,8	499,1	507,5	537,4	531,8	526,6	522,0
1006,5	1040,3	1100,3	1163,2	1213,5	1260,3	1300,1	1363,6	1370,6	1372,7
–	–	–	–	–	–	–	–	68,1	135,9
1821,0	1949,0	1875,0	1791,0	1985,0	2001,0	1946,0	2084,0	1983,0	2066,0

1988	1989	1990	1991	1992	1993	1994[28]	1995	1996	1997
–	24,1	23,4	28,0	–	31,4	34,4	–	36,3	–
34,9	35,2	34,9	37,7	49,6	77,1	103,7	158,6	198,6	210,0
–	–	–	73,9	88,2	–	138,1	140,0	138,0	143,0
–	–	–	–	–	30,0	–	–	70,0	–
–	–	–	–	3,2	2,7	1,9	1,9	1,7	1,4
–	–	–	–	–	–	24,8	48,0	43,0	–
–	–	–	–	–	–	–	171,6	158,5	138,3
–	–	–	–	–	–	–	–	7,1	12,1

14. Numbers of foreigners with annual residence permits (including, up to 31/12/82, holders of permits of durations below 12 months) and holders of settlement permits (permanent permits). Seasonal and frontier workers are excluded. 1993 data from Sopemi. 1994 figure taken in April.
15. Numbers estimated from the annual labour force survey.
16. Provisonal estimate for 1994 figure.
17. 1994 figures from Central Statisitcal Offices etc. in the 1995 reports to the OECD by the individual country SOPEMI Correspondents.
18. 1995 and 1996 figures come from the Council of Europe's Recent Demographic Developments in Europe, 1997.
19. Data as of 31/12 of year indicated are extracted from population registers.
20. Permanently resident foreigners, Ministry of Interior. 1990 figure from Council of Europe (Nov 1994).
21. Data derived from Ministries of Labour and Interior, and include only those holding permanent and long-term residence permits.
22. Temporary residence permit holders only.
23. 1993 figure from IOM (April 1994) – Foreign nationals with permanent residence permits. 1996 figure estimate by Okolski.
24. Foreign citizens with permanent residence permits (granted before 1990). 80,900 had temporary residence in 1996.
25. 1995 and 1996 figures come from the Council of Europe's Recent Demographic Developments in Europe, 1997 or reports to the OECD by the individual country SOPEMI Correspondents.
26. Only permanent resident foreigners, Ministry of Interior, 1998.
27. Central Statistical Bureau of Latvia, 1998.
28. 1994, 1995 and 1996 figures come from the Council of Europe's Recent Demographic Developments in Europe, 1997.

Table 3 – Stock of foreign population as a percentage of total population in selected European countries, 1980-1997[1] (%)

A – Western Europe

	1980	1981	1982	1983	1984	1985	1986	1987
Austria[2]	3,7	3,9	4,0	3,9	3,9	4,0	4,2	4,3
Belgium[3]	–	9,0	9,0	9,0	9,1	8,6	8,6	8,7
Denmark[4]	2,0	2,0	2,0	2,0	2,1	2,3	2,5	2,7
Finland[5]	0,3	0,3	0,3	0,3	0,3	0,3	0,4	0,4
France[6]	–	–	6,8	–	–	6,8	–	–
Germany[7]	7,2	7,5	7,6	7,4	7,1	7,2	7,4	7,6
Greece[8]	2,2	2,3	2,3	2,4	2,4	2,3	2,2	2,2
Ireland[9, 13]	–	–	–	–	–	–	–	–
Italy[10]	0,5	0,6	0,6	0,7	0,7	0,7	0,8	1,0
Luxembourg[18]	25,8	26,1	26,2	26,3	26,5	26,7	26,2	26,5
Netherlands	3,7	3,8	3,8	3,8	3,9	3,8	3,9	4,0
Norway[11]	2,0	2,1	2,2	2,3	2,4	2,4	2,6	2,9
Portugal[12, 13]	0,5	0,5	0,6	0,7	0,7	0,8	0,9	0,9
Spain[13]	0,5	0,5	0,5	0,5	0,6	0,6	0,8	0,9
Sweden[14]	5,1	5,0	4,9	4,8	4,7	4,6	4,7	4,8
Switzerland[15]	14,1	14,3	14,4	14,4	14,4	14,5	14,7	14,9
Turkey	–	–	–	–	–	–	0.04	–
United Kingdom[16]	–	–	–	–	2,8	3,0	3,2	3,2

B – Central and eastern Europe[20] [29]

	1980	1981	1982	1983	1984	1985	1986	1987
Bulgaria[21]	–	–	–	–	–	–	–	–
Czech Republic[22]	–	–	–	–	–	–	–	0,3
Hungary[23]	–	–	–	–	–	–	–	–
Poland[24]	–	–	–	–	–	–	–	–
Romania[25]	–	–	–	–	–	–	–	–
Slovenia[6]	–	–	–	–	–	–	–	–
Russia[27]	–	–	–	–	–	–	–	–
Latvia[28]	–	–	–	–	–	–	–	–

1. Data as of 31/12 of year indicated extracted, except for France, U.K. and otherwise indicated, from population registers.
2. 1983 to 1993 data from Sopemi (1994)
3. In 1985, as a consequence of a modification of the nationality code, some persons who formerly would have been counted as foreigners were included as nationals. This led to a marked decrease in the foreign population. The decrease in 1995 is mainly the result of the effects of changes in nationality laws and removal from the register of asylum seekers awaiting a decision. Source: Eurostat (1994) and Sopemi (1994, 1997)
4. Source: Eurostat (1994) and Sopemi (1994)
5. Source: Central statistical office of Finland. 1994 data to 30th June.
6. Population censuses on 4/3/82 and 6/3/90. The figure for the census of 20/2/75 is 3442.4.
7. Germany refers to the FRG. From 1991, this includes the five new Länder of the former GDR. Data as of 31/10 up to 1984 and in 1990 and as of 31/12 for all other years.
8. Source: NSSG (1994)
9. Department of Justice, annual returns, (excludes U.K. citizens). 1995 figure from report to OECD from Irish SOPEMI correspondent.
10. Data are adjusted to take account of the regularisations which occurred in 1987-88 and 1990. The fall in numbers for 1989 results from a review of the foreigners' register (removing duplicate registrations, accounting for returns). Source: Ministry of the Interior, elaborated by CENSIS.
11. From 1987, asylum seekers whose requests are being processed are included. Numbers for earlier years were fairly small.
12. Source: Serviço de Estrangeiros e Fronteiras. 1993 figure includes estimated 39,200 from special regularisation.
13. Eurostat (1994) and Sopemi (1994)

1988	1989	1990	1991	1992	1993	1994[17]	1995[18]	1996	1997
4,5	5,1	5,9	6,8	7,9	8,6	8,9	9,0	9,0	9,1
8,8	8,9	9,1	9,2	9,0	9,1	9,1	9,0	8,9	8,9
2,8	2,9	3,1	3,3	3,5	3,6	3,8	4,2	4,5	4,5
0,4	0,4	0,5	0,7	0,9	1,0	1,2	1,3	1,4	1,6
–	–	6,3	6,3	–	–	–	–	–	–
7,3	7,7	8,2	7,3	8,0	8,5	8,6	8,8	8,9	–
2,2	2,2	2,3	2,5	2,5	2,6	–	1,5	1,5	1,5
–	0,7	0,8	0,8	2,7	2,7	2,7	2,7	3,2	3,1
1,1	0,9	1,4	1,6	1,6	1,7	1,6	1,7	1,9	2,2
26,8	27,4	28,6	29,4	30,3	31,1	32,0	32,6	33,4	34,1
4,2	4,3	4,6	4,8	5,0	5,1	5,0	5,0	4,3	4,5
3,2	3,3	3,4	3,5	3,6	3,8	3,8	3,7	3,6	3,6
1,0	1,0	1,1	1,2	1,2	1,7	1,6	1,6	1,7	1,7
0,9	1,0	1,0	0,9	1,0	1,1	1,2	1,2	1,4	1,5
5,0	5,3	5,6	5,7	5,7	5,8	6,1	6,0	5,9	5,9
15,2	15,6	16,3	17,0	17,6	18,1	18,6	19,3	19,6	19,4
–	–	–	–	–	–	–	–	0,1	0,2
3,2	3,4	3,3	3,1	3,4	3,4	3,5	3,6	3,4	3,5

1988[29]	1989	1990	1991	1992	1993	1994	1995	1996	1997
–	0,3	0,3	0,3	–	–	–	–	0,4	–
0,3	0,3	0,3	0,4	0,5	0,7	1,0	1,5	1,9	2,0
–	–	–	0,7	0,9	–	1,3	1,4	1,4	1,4
–	–	–	–	–	0,1	–	–	0,2	–
–	–	–	–	0,0	0,0	0,0	0,0	0,0	0,0
–	–	–	–	–	–	1,3	2,4	2,2	2,1
–	–	–	–	–	–	–	0,1	0,1	0,1
–	–	–	–	–	–	–	–	0,3	0,5

14. Some foreigners permits of short duration are not counted (mainly citizens of other Nordic countries).
15. Numbers of foreigners with annual residence permits (including, up to 31/12/82, holders of permits of durations below 12 months) and holders of settlement permits (permanent permits). Seasonal and frontier workers are excluded. 1993 data from Sopemi.
16. Numbers estimated from the annual labour force survey.
17. 1994 data from Central Statistical Offices etc, in the 1995 reports to the OECD by the individual country SOPEMI Correspondents.
18. 1994 percentage based on a provisional estimate absolute value.
19. 1995 and 1996 figures come from the Council of Europe's Recent Demographic Developments in Europe, 1997.
20. Data as of 31/12 of year indicated are extracted from population registers.
21. Permanently resident foreigners, Ministry of Interior. 1990 figure from Council of Europe (Nov 1994).
22. Data derived from Ministries of Labour and Interior, and include only those holding permanent and long-term residence permits.
23. Temporary residence permit holders only.
24. 1993 figure from IOM (April 1994) - Foreign nationals with permanent residence permits.
25. 1992 census
26. 1994, 1995 and 1996 figures come from the Council of Europe's Recent Demographic Developments in Europe, 1997.
27. Only permanent resident foreigners, Ministry of Interior, 1998.
28. Central Statistical Bureau of Latvia, 1998.
29. 1995 and 1996 figures come from the Council of Europe's Recent Demographic Developments in Europe, 1997 or reports to the OECD by the individual country SOPEMI Correspondents.

Table 4 – Inflows of foreign population to selected European countries,
1980-1997[1, 2] (thousands)

A – Western Europe

	1980	1981	1982	1983	1984	1985	1986	1987
Belgium	46,8	41,3	36,2	34,3	37,2	37,5	39,3	40,1
Denmark[10]	14,5	14,5	15,3	16,0	18,0	24,6	26,6	23,8
Finland[10]	1,9	2,3	2,4	2,8	2,7	2,6	2,7	2,8
France[3]	59,4	75,0	144,4	64,2	51,4	43,4	38,3	39,0
Germany[10]	632,3	502,0	322,4	276,4	333,3	400,0	479,5	473,3
Greece [10]	–	–	–	–	–	–	–	–
Iceland	0,4	0,5	0,5	0,6	0,5	0,5	0,6	1,0
Ireland[11]	–	–	–	–	–	–	–	17,2
Italy[4]	88,3	91,5	100,1	98,3	86,9	82,2	75,7	104,5
Luxembourg [10]	7,4	6,9	6,4	6,2	6,0	6,6	7,4	8,3
Netherlands	79,8	50,4	40,9	36,4	37,3	46,2	52,8	60,9
Norway[5]	11,8	13,1	14,0	13,1	12,8	14,9	16,5	23,8
Portugal	–	–	–	–	–	–	–	–
Spain[6, 10]	3,0	11,3	2,8	3,6	4,4	6,2	4,3	5,3
Sweden[7]	34,4	27,4	25,1	22,3	26,1	27,9	34,0	37,1
Switzerland[8]	70,5	80,3	74,7	58,3	58,6	59,4	66,8	71,5
United Kingdom[9]	107,0	93,0	104,0	108,0	106,0	122,0	130,0	113,0

B – Central and eastern Europe[13]

	1980	1981	1982	1983	1984	1985	1986	1987
Czech Republic[14]	–	–	–	–	–	–	–	–
Hungary[5]	–	–	–	–	–	–	–	–
Poland[16]	–	–	–	–	–	–	–	–
Estonia [17]	–	–	–	–	–	–	–	–
Latvia[17]	–	–	–	–	–	–	–	–
Lithuania[17]	–	–	–	–	–	–	–	–
Romania[18]	–	–	–	–	–	–	–	–
Slovak Republic	–	–	–	–	–	–	–	–
"FYR Macedonia	–	–	–	–	–	–	–	–
Russia[19]	–	–	–	–	–	–	–	–
Croatia	–	–	–	–	–	–	–	–

1. Asylum seekers are excluded.
2. The source used for each country is the National Statistical Institute unless otherwise indicated.
3. Entries of new foreign workers, including holders of provisional work permits (APT) and foreigners admitted on family reunification grounds. Does not include residents of EU countries (workers and family members) who have not been processed via the International Migration Office (OMI). 1993 figure rounded to the nearest '000.
4. 1980-1991 – new entries in the population register. 1992 data from Sopemi National Reports (1993).
5. Entries of foreigners intending to stay longer than six months in Norway.
6. Instituto Nacional de Estadistica (INE).
7. Some short duration entries are not counted (mainly citizens of other Nordic countries).
8. Entries of foreigners with annual residence permits, and those with settlement permits (permanent permits) who return to Switzerland after a temporary stay abroad. Includes, up to 31 December 1982, holders of permits of durations below 12 months. Seasonal and frontier workers (including seasonal workers who obtain permanent permits) are excluded. Transformations are excluded.
9. Source: International Passenger Survey, OPCS. 1993 and '94 figures rounded to the nearest '000.
10. 1993 data Eurostat (1995)

[12]

1988	1989	1990	1991	1992	1993	1994	1995	1996	1997
38,2	43,5	50,4	54,1	55,1	53,0	56,0	53,1	51,9	–
22,1	24,4	26,2	29,2	29,1	28,2	28,9	45,9	31,5	–
3,2	4,2	6,5	13,2	10,4	10,9	7,6	7,3	7,5	8,1
44,0	53,2	63,1	65,3	–	116,0	82,8	68,0	74,0	–
648,6	770,8	842,4	920,5	1208,0	989,8	773,9	792,7	707,9	615,3
–	–	25,0	13,4	–	16,3	–	–	22,2	–
1,8	1,0	1,1	1,7	1,0	0,9	–	–	1,3	–
19,2	26,7	33,3	33,3	40,9	35,0	31,5	–	21,5	–
85,8	81,2	96,7	70,9	72,3	–	–	31,0	–	–
9,0	9,1	10,3	10,9	10,7	10,1	10,1	10,3	10,0	10,4
58,3	65,4	81,3	84,3	83,0	87,6	68,4	67,0	77,0	76,7
23,0	18,4	15,7	16,1	17,2	22,3	17,9	16,5	17,2	22,0
–	–	–	–	13,7	9,9	–	–	3,6	–
9,7	14,4	13,7	10,6	18,2	15,4	18,6	19,5	16,7	–
44,5	58,9	53,2	43,9	39,5	54,8	74,7	36,1	29,3	33,0
76,1	80,4	101,4	109,8	112,1	104,0	91,7	87,9	74,3	–
127,0	146,0	161,0	150,0	116,4	120,0	133,0	154,0	168,0	188,0

1988	1989	1990	1991	1992	1993	1994	1995	1996	1997
–	0,7	12,4	14,1	19,1	12,9	10,2	10,5	10,9	12,8
–	33,7	37,1	22,8	14,8	15,9	12,8	13,2	12,5	–
–	2,2	2,6	5,0	6,5	5,9	6,9	8,1	8,2	8,4
–	12,5	8,4	5,2	3,5	2,4	1,6	1,6	1,6	1,6
–	40,3	32,3	14,7	6,2	4,1	3,0	2,8	–	–
–	47,4	38,6	14,2	6,7	2,9	1,7	2,0	3,0	2,5
–	–	–	1,6	1,8	1,3	0,9	4,5	2,1	6,6
–	–	–	–	–	–	–	3,0	2,5	–
–	–	–	–	–	1,5	1,8	1,0	0,6	0,6
–	989,7	1036,3	806,0	1011,3	979,3	1191,4	866,3	647,0	597,7
–	–	–	10,1	48,3	57,7	33,4	42,0	44,6	–

11. Source: CSO (1994) Annual Population and Migration Estimates, 1988-1995, in the 1995 report to the OECD by the Irish SOPEMI Correspondent. The figures for 1992-1994 are provisional and may be subject to revision when the 1996 Census reults are available.
12. 1994 and 1995 figures from reports to the OECD by the individual country SOPEMI Correpondents.
13. Asylum seekers are excluded.
14. Immigrants are persons who have been granted a permanent residence permit. 1994 figure from the Czech Statistical Office, in the 1995 report to the OECD by the Czech SOPEMI Correspondent. Includes those from Slovak Republic (1990 onwards).
15. Source: KEOKH, in the 1996 report to the OECD by the Hungarian SOPEMI Correspondent.
16. Immigrants are persons granted a permanent residence permit. Numbers may be underestimates since not all children accompanying immigrants are registered.
17. Recorded as "external" migration flows referring to non-Baltic countries. From 1996 report to the OECD by the Baltic States' correspondent. Flows of Nationals included.
18. Persons granted a permanent residence permit.
19. Source: State Committee on Statistics, 1998.

Annex II

State of ratification of relevant Europe Conventions

United Nations

International Convention relating to the Status of Refugees (1951)

International Convention on the Elimination of all Forms of Racial Discrimination (1965)

International Convention on the Protection of All Migrant Workers and Members of their Family (1990)

International Convention on the Rights of the Child (1989)

Website: http://untreaty.un.org/

ILO Convention on Migrant Workers (Supplementary Provisions) (1975)

ILO Convention on Discrimination (Employment and Occupation) (1960)

ILO Convention on Indigenous and Tribal People (1989)

Website: http://www.ilolex.ilo.ch:1567/public/

Council of Europe legal instruments:

Convention for the Protection of Human Rights and Fundamental Freedoms and protocols to the said Convention (includes Nos. 9, 44, 45, 46, 55, 114, 117, 118, 140) (1991) (ETS 5)

European Convention on Establishment (1977), (ETS 19)

European Social Charter and Additional Protocol (1990), (ETS 35 and 128)

European Social Charter (revised) (1996), (ETS 163)

European Convention on the Legal Status of Migrant Workers (1985), (ETS 93)

Framework Convention for the Protection of National Minorities (Strasbourg, 1995) (1995), (ETS 157)

European Cultural Convention (1982), (ETS 18)

European Charter for Regional or Minority Languages (Strasbourg, 1992) (1993), (ETS 148)

European Convention on the Reduction of Cases of Multiple Nationality and Military Obligations in Cases of Multiple Nationality (1994), (ETS 43)

European Convention on Nationality (1997), (ETS 166)

Convention on the Participation of Foreigners in Public Life at Local Level (Strasbourg, 1992), (ETS 144)

Website: http://conventions.coe.int/treaty/FR/cadreprincipal.htm

Annex II

State of ratification of relevant European Conventions

Annex III

List of publications on Community relations

Titles in the series "Community relations" :

Police training concerning migrants and ethnic relations, Practical guidelines, 1994
(ISBN 92-871-2459-0)

Tackling racism and xenophobia: practical action at the local level, 1995
(ISBN 92-871-2695-X)

Vocational training projects: towards equal opportunities, 1994 (ISBN 92-871-2568-6)

Immigrant women and integration, 1995 (ISBN 92-871-2834-0)

The role of management and trade unions in promoting equal opportunities in employment, 1996 (ISBN 92-871-3039-6)

Tackling racist and xenophobic violence in Europe: review and practical guidance,
Robin Oakley, 1996 (ISBN 92-871-3037-X)

Area-based projects in districts of high immigrant concentration, 1996
(ISBN 92-871-3179-1)

Tackling racist and xenophobic violence in Europe: case studies, 1997
(ISBN 92-871-3483-9)

Measurement and indicators of integration, 1997 (ISBN 92-871-3498-7)

Initiatives by employers to promote employment and integration of immigrants,
1998 (ISBN 92-871-3786-2)

Security of residence of long-term migrants: a comparative study of law and practice in European countries by Kees Groenendijk, Elspeth Guild and Halil Dogan, 1998
(ISBN 92-871-3788-9)

Political and social participation of immigrants through consultative bodies, 1999
(ISBN 92-871-3891-5)

Religion and the integration of immigrants, 1999 (ISBN 92-871-4041-3)

Strategies for implementing integration policies – Proceedings (Prague, 4-6 May 1999)
[CDMG (2000) 8]

Annex IV

List of activites undertaken to prepare this report

I. *Editorial Group (MG-ED)*

Six meetings were held on the following dates:

- 29/30 April 1998
- 04/06 November 1998
- 24/26 February 1999
- 17/18 June 1999
- 14/15 October 1999
- 16/17 December 1999

The European Committee on Migration (CDMG) was consulted at every stage of elaboration of the draft report. It adopted the final version at its 42nd meeting held in Strasbourg from 3 to 5 May 2000.

List of members of the Editorial Group

France

Mme **Nadia MAROT**, Chef du Bureau des affaires internationales, Direction de la Population et des Migrations, Ministère de l'Emploi et de la Solidarité, 8 avenue de Ségur, F-75350 PARIS 07SP
Tel.: + 33 1 40 56 40 05. Fax: + 33 1 40 56 50 42.
E-mail: Nadia.Marot@sante.gouv.fr

Hungary

Ms Éva HEGYESINE ORSÓS, Terez krt. 6, H-1066 BUDAPEST VI
Tel.: +36 1 321 39 66 – Fax: +36 1 351 60 31 – E-mail: orsoseva@mail.matav.hu

Italy

Ms Vaifra PALANCA, Ministry of Social Affairs, Via Veneto 56, I-00186 ROME
Tel: +39 6 48 16 14 29; Fax: +39 6 48 16 14 73 – E-mail: palanca@affarisociali.it

Netherlands

Mr Jacques P. VEERIS, Kersengaarde 258, NL-2272 NN VOORBURG
Tel.: +31 70 3270992 – E-mail: jpveeris@bart.nl

Norway

Ms Litt-Woon LONG, Sverdrupsg. 5, N-0559 OSLO
Tel.: +47 22 37 06 64 – E-mail:litt-woon.long@deloitte.no

Poland

Mr Tomasz Kuba KOZLOWSKI
Institute of Public Affairs, ul. Mikolaja Reja 7 – 00-922-WARSAW 54
Tel.: +48 22 825 59 07 – Fax: +48 22 825 53 05 – e-mail: kuba@isp.org.pl

Russian Federation

Mrs Natalia VORONINA, Leader Researcher, Institute of Ethnology and
Anthropology, Russian Academy of Sciences, RUS-MOSCOW
Tel./Fax: +7 095 924 23 92 – E-mail: nvoronina@glasnet.ru

United Kingdom

Ms Mary COUSSEY, Senior Research Associate, Judge Institute of Management
Studies, University of Cambridge, The Lodge, Clare College,
GB – CAMBRIDGE CR2 1TL
Tel: 44 1223 328 168 – Fax: 44 1223 333 249 – E-mail: mc215@cam.ac.uk

Consultants

Mr Jan NIESSEN, Director
Migration Policy Group (MPG), 205 rue Belliard, Box 1, B-1040 BRUXELLES
Tel.: +32 2 230 59 30 – Fax: +32 2 280 09 25 – E-mail: jniessen@compuserve.com

Ms Lori LINDBURG, Senior Research Associate,
Migration Policy Group (MPG), 205 rue Belliard, Box 1, B-1040 BRUXELLES
Tel.: +32 2 230 59 30 – Fax: +32 2 280 09 25

Ms Christina WILLE, Research Associate
Migration Policy Group (MPG), 205 rue Belliard, Box 1, B-1040 BRUXELLES
Tel.: +32 2 230 59 30 – Fax: +32 2 280 09 25

Secretariat

Mme Maria OCHOA-LLIDO, Chef de la Division des migrations et des
Roms/Tsiganes
Tel: +33 (0)3 88 41 21 79 – Fax: +33 (0)3 88 41 27 31
E-mail: maria.ochoa-llido@ coe.int

Mme Eva KOPROLIN, Administratrice
Division des migrations et des Roms/Tsiganes
Tel: +33 (0)3 88 41 29 24 – Fax: +33 (0)3 88 41 27 31
E-mail: eva.koprolin@ coe.int

Mme Isabelle CHANEL, Secrétaire
Division des migrations et des Roms/Tsiganes
Tel. +33 (0)3 88 41 21 66 – Fax: +33 (0)3 88 41 27 31
E-mail: isabelle.chanel@ coe.int

Hearing with experts on 24 February 1999

A hearing was held during the third meeting of the Drafting Group (MG-ED) with the afore-mentioned experts, thanks to the financial contribution from the European Cultural Foundation. This exchange of views was enriching for the contents of the report.

Dr Eva Maria BLUM, Amt für Multikulturelle Angelegenheiten,
Walter Kolb Strasse, 9-11, – D-60594 FRANKFURT
Tel.: +49 69 212 38765 – Fax: + 49 69 212 37946

Prof Marco MARTINIELLO, Chercheur qualifié FNRS et maitre de conférences, Université de Liège, Faculté de Droit – Science Politique, Centre d'Etudes des Migrations et de l'Ethnicité (CEDEM) Batiment 31,Boite 38, 7, Boulevard du Rectorat, B-4000 LIEGE (Sart-Tilman)
Tel.: + 32 4 366 30 40 – Fax: +32 4 366 45 57 – E-mail: M.Martiniello@ulg.ac.be

Mr Ivan VEJVODA, Executive Director, Fund for an Open Society, Zmaj Jovina 34, 11000 BELGRADE, YUGOSLAVIA
Tel.: +381 11 3283076 – Fax: +381 11 3283602
E-mail: ivejvoda@sfj.opennet.org

Ms Veronie WILLEMARS, Grants Officer, European Cultural Foundation,
Jan van Goyenkade 5, – NL-1075 HN AMSTERDAM
Tel.: +31 20 6760222 – Fax: +31 20 6752231 – E-mail: vwillemars@eurocult.org

II. *National Round Tables in newer countries of immigration organised with the Migration Policy Group in co-operation with the European Cultural Foundation.*

Since the Warsaw Conference in 1996, the CDMG has organised, in collaboration with the Migration Policy Group, national round tables on integration and community relations policy. Such events are held in countries of recent immigration (mainly in Southern, Central and Eastern Europe) where the development of integration policy is still at a fairly early stage. The countries concerned have found the round tables to be an effective way of initiating a process of dialogue between all those concerned with integration policy.

In 1998 and 1999, Round tables have been held in: Bulgaria, Czech Republic, Greece, Hungary, Poland, Romania, Slovakia, Finland, Lithuania, Russia, Slovenia, Ukraine and Albania.

Sales agents for publications of the Council of Europe
Agents de vente des publications du Conseil de l'Europe

AUSTRALIA/AUSTRALIE
Hunter Publications, 58A, Gipps Street
AUS-3066 COLLINGWOOD, Victoria
Tel.: (61) 3 9417 5361
Fax: (61) 3 9419 7154
E-mail: Sales@hunter-pubs.com.au
http://www.hunter-pubs.com.au

AUSTRIA/AUTRICHE
Gerold und Co., Graben 31
A-1011 WIEN 1
Tel.: (43) 1 533 5014
Fax: (43) 1 533 5014 18
E-mail: buch@gerold.telecom.at
http://www.gerold.at

BELGIUM/BELGIQUE
La Librairie européenne SA
50, avenue A. Jonnart
B-1200 BRUXELLES 20
Tel.: (32) 2 734 0281
Fax: (32) 2 735 0860
E-mail: info@libeurop.be
http://www.libeurop.be

Jean de Lannoy
202, avenue du Roi
B-1190 BRUXELLES
Tel.: (32) 2 538 4308
Fax: (32) 2 538 0841
E-mail: jean.de.lannoy@euronet.be
http://www.jean-de-lannoy.be

CANADA
Renouf Publishing Company Limited
5369 Chemin Canotek Road
CDN-OTTAWA, Ontario, K1J 9J3
Tel.: (1) 613 745 2665
Fax: (1) 613 745 7660
E-mail: order.dept@renoufbooks.com
http://www.renoufbooks.com

CZECH REPUBLIC/
RÉPUBLIQUE TCHÈQUE
USIS, Publication Service
Havelkova 22
CZ-130 00 PRAHA 3
Tel./Fax: (420) 2 2423 1114

DENMARK/DANEMARK
Munksgaard
35 Norre Sogade, PO Box 173
DK-1005 KØBENHAVN K
Tel.: (45) 7 733 3333
Fax: (45) 7 733 3377
E-mail: direct@munksgaarddirect.dk
http://www.munksgaarddirect.dk

FINLAND/FINLANDE
Akateeminen Kirjakauppa
Keskuskatu 1, PO Box 218
FIN-00381 HELSINKI
Tel.: (358) 9 121 41
Fax: (358) 9 121 4450
E-mail: akatilaus@stockmann.fi
http://www.akatilaus.akateeminen.com

FRANCE
C.I.D.
131 boulevard Saint-Michel
F-75005 PARIS
Tel.: (33) 01 43 54 47 15
Fax: (33) 01 43 54 80 73
E-mail: cid@msh-paris.fr

GERMANY/ALLEMAGNE
UNO Verlag
Proppelsdorfer Allee 55
D-53115 BONN
Tel.: (49) 2 28 94 90 231
Fax: (49) 2 28 21 74 92
E-mail: unoverlag@aol.com
http://www.uno-verlag.de

GREECE/GRÈCE
Librairie Kauffmann
Mavrokordatou 9
GR-ATHINAI 106 78
Tel.: (30) 1 38 29 283
Fax: (30) 1 38 33 967

HUNGARY/HONGRIE
Euro Info Service
Hungexpo Europa Kozpont ter 1
H-1101 BUDAPEST
Tel.: (361) 264 8270
Fax: (361) 264 8271
E-mail: euroinfo@euroinfo.hu
http://www.euroinfo.hu

ITALY/ITALIE
Libreria Commissionaria Sansoni
Via Duca di Calabria 1/1, CP 552
I-50125 FIRENZE
Tel.: (39) 556 4831
Fax: (39) 556 41257
E-mail: licosa@licosa.com
http://www.licosa.com

NETHERLANDS/PAYS-BAS
De Lindeboom Internationale Publikaties
PO Box 202, MA de Ruyterstraat 20 A
NL-7480 AE HAAKSBERGEN
Tel.: (31) 53 574 0004
Fax: (31) 53 572 9296
E-mail: lindeboo@worldonline.nl
http://home-1-worldonline.nl/~lindeboo/

NORWAY/NORVÈGE
Akademika, A/S Universitetsbokhandel
PO Box 84, Blindern
N-0314 OSLO
Tel.: (47) 22 85 30 30
Fax: (47) 23 12 24 20

POLAND/POLOGNE
Głowna Księgarnia Naukowa
im. B. Prusa
Krakowskie Przedmiescie 7
PL-00-068 WARSZAWA
Tel.: (48) 29 22 66
Fax: (48) 22 26 64 49
E-mail: inter@internews.com.pl
http://www.internews.com.pl

PORTUGAL
Livraria Portugal
Rua do Carmo, 70
P-1200 LISBOA
Tel.: (351) 13 47 49 82
Fax: (351) 13 47 02 64
E-mail: liv.portugal@mail.telepac.pt

SPAIN/ESPAGNE
Mundi-Prensa Libros SA
Castelló 37
E-28001 MADRID
Tel.: (34) 914 36 37 00
Fax: (34) 915 75 39 98
E-mail: libreria@mundiprensa.es
http://www.mundiprensa.com

SWITZERLAND/SUISSE
BERSY
Route d'Uvrier 15
CH-1958 LIVRIER/SION
Tel.: (41) 27 203 73 30
Fax: (41) 27 203 73 32
E-mail: bersy@freesurf.ch

UNITED KINGDOM/ROYAUME-UNI
TSO (formerly HMSO)
51 Nine Elms Lane
GB-LONDON SW8 5DR
Tel.: (44) 171 873 8372
Fax: (44) 171 873 8200
E-mail: customer.services@theso.co.uk
http://www.the-stationery-office.co.uk
http://www.itsofficial.net

UNITED STATES and CANADA/
ÉTATS-UNIS et CANADA
Manhattan Publishing Company
468 Albany Post Road, PO Box 850
CROTON-ON-HUDSON,
NY 10520, USA
Tel.: (1) 914 271 5194
Fax: (1) 914 271 5856
E-mail: Info@manhattanpublishing.com
http://www.manhattanpublishing.com

STRASBOURG
Librairie Kléber
Palais de l'Europe
F-67075 STRASBOURG Cedex
Fax: (33) 03 88 52 91 21

Council of Europe Publishing/Editions du Conseil de l'Europe
F-67075 Strasbourg Cedex
Tel.: (33) 03 88 41 25 81 – Fax: (33) 03 88 41 39 10
E-mail: publishing@coe.int – Web site: http://book.coe.fr